DEATH OF A LAW FIRM

Staying Strong in the Global Legal Market

JAAP BOSMAN
WITH LISA HAKANSON

Cover design by Elmarie Jara/ABA Design

Printed in the United States of America.

21 20 19 18 17 5 4 3 2 1

Library of Congress Cataloging-in-Publication Data
Names: Bosman, Jaap, author. | Hakanson, Lisa, author.
Title: Death of a law firm : why many business law firms will collapse in the next five years / by Jaap Bosman ; co-written by Lisa Hakanson.
Description: Chicago : American Bar Association, 2017. | Includes index.
Identifiers: LCCN 2017018273 | ISBN 9781634258494 | ISBN 1634258495
Subjects: LCSH: Law firms—United States. | Practice of law—United States. | Commercial law—United States.
Classification: LCC KF318 .B67 2017 | DDC 338.4/7340973—dc23
LC record available at https://lccn.loc.gov/2017018273

CONTENTS

PREFACE

For decades, the business of law has been one of the most profitable business models. Earnings and returns on investment are among the highest in the market. Many partners make more money than elected heads of state and have earnings that are comparable to those of CEOs of sizable companies. Clearly, the business of law has been doing something right.

Decade after decade, partner income has been steadily growing. Only the 2008 global financial crisis managed to cause a little dip. Almost every law firm circumvented this dip by quickly initiating cost-cutting operations. Because of these measures, most law firms even managed to increase profits beyond the precrisis levels.

Cutting costs, however, is a purely cosmetic solution—a matter of hygiene that improves the results without improving the underlying business. Applying cosmetics, therefore, can be dangerous.

The international legal landscape has been changing significantly over the last decade. We witnessed the rise of omnipresent international business law firms; we saw new alternative legal service providers enter the market. The Big Four accountants are setting up legal services arms that are becoming a factor to be reckoned with. In-house departments have become stronger, better qualified, and better organized than ever before. All of these developments create increased competition in the market.

One factor that will have a more fundamental impact than any other on the business of law is *commoditization*—the silent killer that will cause the death of many law firms. Commoditization arises when, from the client's perspective, multiple law firms and multiple lawyers can perform the same task equally well. Commoditization does not equal simple work or bulk work, as we are sometimes led to believe.

On the contrary, commoditized legal work can be quite complicated and require a high level of skills. It is the mere fact that many lawyers have the same skills that will make a certain type of work a commodity. Invariably, lawyers suffer from "commoditization blindness," denying that their work is commoditized. This denial makes the issue even more severe. Commoditization will inevitably lead to pressure on price, whether it is by clients demanding lower rates or by pushing work down (handing it to a less-expensive law firm). Due to its eroding effect on profits, commoditization is the single-most important disrupting factor in the legal market today. This book is the first to raise awareness to the potentially devastating effects of commoditization.

Dark clouds are building heavily behind us in the sky. When the right measures are taken, it is perfectly possible not only to survive the storm but to come out even stronger than before. To compensate for the eroding effect of commoditization, all law firms have to do is change their business model. However simple it might seem, changing a business model might be one bridge too far for most firms. As this book argues, the inner workings of law firm partnerships are rigged against change. In reading this book, you will gain an unprecedented insight into the psychology of the partner group—or maybe even a confronting look in the mirror.

The good news is that the global legal market will continue to grow. We are not in a shrinking market. The players in the market, however, will be significantly reshuffled in the next five years, leading to the rise of some and to the death of others. Read the book and make sure your firm ends up in the right category.

Jaap Bosman

1

ICARUS'S FALL

In May 2001, I made my first visit to Los Angeles. I was staying at the Beverly Wilshire Hotel at the end of Rodeo Drive where *Pretty Woman* had been filmed a few years earlier. During the hour-long drive from the airport to my hotel, I struggled to find any glamour. Looking out of the window of my taxi, I dismissed Los Angeles as one of the uglier and more run-down cities I had seen. A feeling of dreariness settled in as nothing but low, square concrete boxes, devoid of charm and character, lined the streets along the way. It felt like the Los Angeles riots had taken place the week before. As it turned out, the California electricity crisis was at its peak during my visit, and we were plunged into darkness on a few occasions by power outages. Failing power supply in a first-world country instills one with a sense of doom.

The next day, I had reasons to adjust my assessment. The steel-and-glass buildings of downtown Los Angeles, its sharp-suited inhabitants and suave business clubs, stood in a poignant juxtaposition to the lackluster city surrounding it. At the time, the law firm I was with had an office in Singapore, which entitled us to membership of the Pacific Rim Advisory Council (PRAC), a strategic alliance between top-tier law firms in the broader Pacific Rim region. My reason for going to Los Angeles was to attend PRAC's 29th International Conference, hosted by Brobeck, Phleger & Harrison.

The headquarters were situated in a brand-new, shiny glass-and-steel structure that did what it was supposed to do: embody success and strike awe in its visitors.

Brobeck, Phleger & Harrison was a 77-year-old blue-chip firm based in San Francisco, California. At the time of my visit, the firm consisted of 754 attorneys spread over eight offices, and its profits per partner had soared to more than $1 million a year. It was a thoroughbred law firm formed in 1926 by three lawyers from Morrison & Foerster (then Morrison, Dunne & Brobeck) who spent the following decades building up a portfolio of A-list clients based in the San Francisco area. Managing partner Herman Phleger served as an advisor to Bernard Baruch during the creation of the United Nations in the 1940s. In 1980, the firm established an office in Palo Alto to serve expanding technology companies. By the mid-1990s, Brobeck served clients such as Cisco Systems, Sun Microsystems, Nokia, and Nike. During the dot-com boom between 1998 and 2000, Brobeck's revenue jumped from $214 million to $314 million.

During my visit in May 2001, Brobeck was the perfect host. We were taken to see the new Getty Museum that had been finished a few years earlier. Perched on its hill in the Brentwood neighborhood, it provided views overlooking Los Angeles along with world-class architecture. We were whisked off to lunch at the prestigious California Club situated a stone's throw from Brobeck's headquarters. The California Club is a private club established in 1888 and now situated in the heart of downtown Los Angeles in an Italian Renaissance–style building from 1930. Its membership is exclusive, and although having diversified adequately since the 19th century, the club still conjured images of gentlemen droning on and discussing business while having a drink. In the evening, we were invited to an intimate, luxurious dinner hosted by a partner in his own home. The weather allowed for extensive use of the lush garden, and the evening was the perfect mix of tasteful familiarity and representative pampering.

Although I remember all these details quite vividly, there is one memory that stands out: Tower Snow Jr. One cannot paint a picture of Brobeck in 2001 without also providing a portrait of its charismatic leader. Tower Snow was, and still is, a securities litigator who, as its managing partner, took Brobeck to its soaring heights in the late 1990s and early part of the first decade. He had a strategy of aggressively wooing high-tech clients and going after lateral partners. The firm grew by 40 percent in one year alone. Taking the stage to address the attendees of the PRAC conference was a tall, sharply attired man who oozed confidence, a modern-day Apollo residing in the unattainable heights of a US top-tier business law firm. He delivered a riveting speech on how he saw the future of legal business. The audience hung on his words, in thrall. He painted with the large brush strokes of a gifted visionary and spoke of taking the firm public. A year later, Tower Snow was ousted. He took with him 50 Brobeck lawyers and the firm's death spiral was revealed for all to see. During one of the plenary sessions on the first day, I had given a presentation on branding and positioning of law firms. Later that same day, our host firm proudly presented its unprecedented nationwide television advertisement campaign, which had just been launched, making it the first corporate law firm in the United States to advertise on national television. It was reported that the campaign, which ran on CNN, might have cost $10 million. As it turns out, Tower Snow was more Icarus than Apollo.

Two years after my visit, Brobeck was liquidated after it had been subjected to bankruptcy proceedings through a petition filed by its creditors. The fall of Brobeck was unprecedented. At the time of my visit, such a scenario was unthinkable. Brobeck was sacrosanct. Large law firms of that stature do not collapse. Shock rippled through the legal community when the news broke. A firm that served as a benchmark for corporate law firms worldwide had failed. Why? How?

Brobeck's brief but informative Wikipedia page provides the following summary of its demise:

> When the dot-com bubble burst in 2001 onward, the firm's strategy of betting on technology clients to compensate the firm's lawyers imploded as the lawyers' equity shares became worthless, work dried up and partners with traditional clients or portable business darted to other firms. Chairman Tower Snow was ousted in 2002, and decamped with some 50 Brobeck attorneys to begin the West Coast offices of London-based giant Clifford Chance Rogers & Wells, now called Clifford Chance.[1]

Brobeck engaged in talks to merge with neighboring San Francisco firm Morgan, Lewis & Bockius, but after four months, merger talks broke off on January 29, 2003. Overwhelmed by partner defections, bank debt, and loads of empty office space, Brobeck announced two days later that it was disbanding.

My argument is that Brobeck is not so much the victim of the extraordinary circumstances it was in—the dot-com boom and implosion—as it is the most spectacular example of a law firm that implements an unrealistic strategy. It ascribed itself capabilities it did not have, and although it is certainly not the only law firm to do so, it went far further than any other law firm at that time. Some might argue that lawyers should not be doing business because they are simply not good at it.

The demise of Brobeck was probably not just the result of a case of misguided leadership in the form of Tower Snow, who failed to judge the tech market the firm had honed itself to service. "He believed that a law firm could be run like a successful company and, influenced by clients such as Cisco Systems Inc., he emulated the growth, management, marketing and sheer boldness of Silicon Valley's highfliers."[2] Indeed, Brobeck began to act like its technology clients. Its lawyers began accepting equity from emerging companies in lieu of traditional law firm compensation. Brobeck was one of the two largest firms representing technology start-ups in Silicon Valley, and there was a frenzy of venture capital deals, initial public offerings, and subsequent consolidations.

Making equity investments, though, is another game altogether. It takes a different set of skills than those usually possessed by a lawyer. However, this argument not only is too simplistic but also misses an important point. Brobeck is not a case of a law firm failing because its leader was unskilled in business. It failed partly because he was bad at leading a law firm. There is a vast difference between running a successful business and running a successful law firm. The fall of Brobeck may, at the time, have been unprecedented, but as it later turned out, it was not a standalone event. More firms have followed. This book does not describe them all, but at least 50 larger firms have failed since 2000. The sudden demise of King & Wood Mallesons Europe, along with a handful of preceding failed law firms—Heller Ehrman; Thelen; Dewey & LeBoeuf; Bingham McCutchen; and Howrey—are worth a closer look. Let us start with Howrey.

In 2006, two partners I know well from two different law firms, each with a star practice in intellectual property, decided to join Howrey. At the time, Howrey was seen as an unparalleled global firm for all intellectual property–related matters. It also had one of the highest profits per partner. Neither of the partners joining Howrey was dissatisfied as such with their respective firms, which were both reputable and profitable. Knowing them both well, I can assure you that money was not their primary driver. They simply wanted to work with the best. Profit per partner is not only a number; it is the measure by which the top-tier lawyers keep track of the best people in the business. An ambitious lawyer ranked at the highest tier of his or her field will seek glory rather than just monetary gains.

There is a vast difference between running a successful business and running a successful law firm

In 2009, Howrey appeared to the outside world to be a thriving global enterprise with more than 700 lawyers, reputable clients, and a tight focus on antitrust, intellectual property, and commercial litigation. In that year, it posted an annual turnover of more than half a billion dollars and had a soaring profit per partner of $1.3 million. By the end of 2010, the profit per partner had halved.

The firm was founded as Howrey, Simon, Baker, & Murchison in 1956 by four antitrust attorneys, including Jack Howrey, a former chairman of the Federal Trade Commission. The firm developed a reputation for gloves-off representation that attracted big corporate clients looking to protect themselves from federal regulators. Similar to Brobeck, in the 1990s, Howrey was one of the first major law firms to pursue a branding strategy with a million-dollar media campaign. In times when partnership loyalty was the backbone of every reputable firm, managing partner Ralph Savarese embarked on what was then viewed as an aggressive campaign to lure partners away from rival firms. In 2000, Howrey & Simon merged with Arnold, White & Durkee, an intellectual property firm with 120 attorneys and offices in six cities. This combination resulted in the new firm of Howrey, Simon, Arnold & White. With 350 lawyers, it was one of the largest antitrust and intellectual property practices in the world. This marked the start of Howrey's expansion overseas, led by Ralph Savarese's successor Robert Ruyak. The firm shortened its name to Howrey. Between 2000 and 2008, the firm grew to more than 700 attorneys and had 17 offices in the United States, Europe, and Asia. Howrey's profits per equity partner peaked in 2008, after which it started to decline, first by 35 percent in 2009, then down to 50 percent the following year. In 2010, a group of 60 attorneys left Howrey, and the death spiral had begun. In March 2011, the executive committee announced that Howrey would dissolve.

An ambitious lawyer ranked in the highest tier will seek glory rather than just monetary gains

Several causes are cited as the reasons for Howrey's fate. The firm had taken on high fixed costs, something a litigation firm must be particularly cautious about because revenue in the litigation business tends to be irregular. Howrey was relying heavily on contingency fees, which declined sharply between 2008 and 2009. Corporate clients began demanding lower fees and billing arrangements that were less favorable to Howrey. There was also an increasing problem caused by conflicts of interest. The larger a litigation firm becomes, the more likely it is that it will encounter conflicts of interest and have to turn down clients. Howrey's European offices were experiencing just that—newly hired partners had to abide by the more stringent rules in the United States and subsequently lost their clients. The fast expansion, the excessive overhead, the volatility of revenue, and the conflicts of interest—all of these led to an abrupt drop in profit per partner. It took just two consecutive years of falling profit for the first large partner group to depart. Lawsuits following the collapse suggest that the extent of the firm's financial troubles was not clear to most partners. In Enron style, the law firm was borrowing money against an overestimated future income to fund operations and partner draws. It may well be that partners would have started to depart in droves already in 2009 had they known the true extent of the financial woes. Once the first larger batch of partners leave, the remaining partners will immediately take action to leave for other firms, taking the best deal they can get. Nobody wants to be the last man standing amidst the remnants of a financial mess. The partners at Howrey were no exception, leading to the firm's dissolution a few months after the first group of lawyers had left.

As opposed to the narrow focus of Brobeck and Howrey, the firm Dewey & LeBoeuf had a broad portfolio. It was known for its corporate, insurance, litigation, tax, and restructuring practices. The 2009 *Chambers Global*[3] ranked the firm as a leader in 35 practice areas and named 37 of its lawyers as leading practitioners. Dewey & LeBoeuf certainly was not relying on one or two practice areas, as one could argue that Brobeck and Howrey had done.

Dewey & LeBoeuf was created in 2007 through the combining of two revered New York–based firms: Dewey Ballantine and LeBoeuf, Lamb, Greene & MacRae. The latter had, at that time, approximately 650 attorneys in 19 offices around the world due to an ambitious growth strategy that began in the 1970s and continued through the 1990s. After the merger, the new firm Dewey & LeBoeuf had a fee-earner headcount of more than 1,300 people in 26 offices around the world. It was the largest merger of New York law firms in history. Dewey & LeBoeuf handled high-profile transactions for marquee clients such as JPMorgan Chase in banking, Lloyd's in insurance, BP in energy, Disney in media and entertainment, eBay in technology, and Alcoa in heavy industry. The firm attracted lateral partners by offering corpulent financial packages, and it had some of the highest-paid corporate lawyers in the United States. Yet, a mere five years after the merger, Dewey and LeBoeuf fell to bankruptcy. The *New York Times* called it the largest law firm collapse in US history.[4]

> *It took just two consecutive years of falling profit for the first large partner group to depart*

Just as Brobeck's did, the compensation system of Dewey & LeBoeuf differed from the traditional system in which financial risks and rewards are shared equally among partners and they are paid according to the same lockstep system of compensation and benefits. This system, often called the Cravath system, is attributed to

Paul D. Cravath, the presiding partner at Cravath, Swaine & Moore from 1906 until 1940. LeBoeuf, Lamb, Greene & MacRae, since its inception in 1929, allocated compensation on the basis of individual performance rather than using the lockstep method. The dominant partner, Randall LeBoeuf Jr., provided the foundation for this system. Partners were paid a base compensation supplemented by their share of the firm's profits. To determine the additional compensation, a complicated point system was used involving their success in attracting new clients, hours billed, quality of work and pro-bono activities, and service to the firm. Compensation varied dramatically.

LeBoeuf, Lamb, Greene & MacRae wanted to grow. Before seeking out Dewey Ballantine to merge with, LeBoeuf brought in 22 lateral partners with various signing bonuses and guarantees. Dewey Ballantine was a pedigree New York firm that was ailing financially, but it still had some star partners. An article in *The New Yorker* revealed that during preparations for the merger, Dewey Ballantine was advised by the management consulting firm McKinsey to "create financial incentives for partners to remain at the Firm"[5] because the top 5 percent of partners at LeBoeuf generated 42 percent of the year's billings. This skew made LeBoeuf "vulnerable to the financial risk posed by individual 'rainmakers' leaving the firm."[6] Law firm mergers are often plagued by partner exodus, and headhunters usually descend at the first burgeoning rumor of a merger. The merger with Dewey Ballantine meant issuing payment guarantees so that the key partners would remain with the firm. A number of key partners got contracts for "target" compensation that would be paid out after three years if they remained. When the often-generous terms were leaked among the partners of the merged entity, many started making demands for guarantees of their own. By 2011, there were about a hundred partners with some kind of special agreement.

Dewey & LeBoeuf may have been suffering from Manhattanization. In the United Kingdom, it would be called the *magic circle* syndrome. The so-called white shoe firms centered in Manhattan, such as Cravath, Davis Polk, and Sullivan & Cromwell, become the yardstick against which profit is measured and the benchmark to strive for. *White shoe firm* is a label used for the most prestigious firms in professions such as law, investment banking, and management consulting, generally originating from the US East Coast. The term originates from the use of the "white buck" suede or buckskin oxford shoes that were popular among certain sections of the student population at US Ivy League colleges during the 1950s. Back then, a white shoe firm implied an East Coast firm serving "old money" clientele, allowing only WASPs[7] among its ranks. It initially referred to leading US firms such as J.P. Morgan, Cravath, Swaine & Moore, and McKinsey. Over time, its usage has expanded to denote top-tier firms in the United States, irrespective of their origins or creed, that charge a premium for their services. A small group of the most successful of these law firms are located in Manhattan, close to their Wall Street clients. A law firm has fallen victim of Manhattanization if it strives to attain the success of these law firms while failing to see that it does not belong to this narrow category. It becomes an unrealistic, deadly beacon guiding a firm's strategy. As the financial crisis hit in 2008, income from the M&A and equity capital market practices plummeted for Dewey & LeBoeuf, as it did for most firms. Although other practice areas of the firm, such as the insurance side, were flourishing, these profits would not be enough to cover the generous compensation contracts. Ordinarily, when profits decline, compensation declines, but the compensation contracts, with their guarantees, prevented that. Just like Howrey, the firm started paying its partners by borrowing against future income. But revenues did not pick up. On May 28, 2012, Dewey & LeBoeuf filed for bankruptcy.

A more recent example, similar to Dewey & LeBoeuf, is that of law firm Bingham McCutchen. In 2014, the firm lost more than 50 partners, including 18 partners at its London office. Just before losing these partners, Bingham McCutchen was an international firm with approximately 850 attorneys in nine US offices and five international offices. The firm had been placed among the top five in *Fortune* magazine's ranking of top-paying companies every year since 2006. In 2013, the firm saw revenue drop by $110 million. In late 2014, several hundred of Bingham McCutchen's partners and associate lawyers left to join Philadelphia-based Morgan Lewis. Legal analysts believe the firm's rapid expansion was the source of its troubles. Bingham merged with 10 law firms in fewer than 15 years. As the firm expanded, just like

Dewey & LeBoeuf, it lured rainmakers with multimillion-dollar contract guarantees, which it could not afford. Toward the end of 2014, 266 out of 310 partners from Bingham had joined Morgan Lewis, and Bingham McCutchen ceased to exist.

Dewey & LeBoeuf's—and arguably Bingham McCutchen's—strategy was an insistence upon expansion by all means possible. It adhered to the misguided notion, as did Howrey, that bigger is always better, especially if you get there fast. One could be tempted to conclude from the cases of Brobeck, Howrey, and LeBoeuf that avoiding rapid expansion and being prudent about taking on overhead costs should make a firm more resilient and help it to steer clear of ruin. Another common denominator shared by the three firms was their charismatic leaders combined with a lack of governance. "My firm doesn't have that problem," you might think, deeming it safe as a result. Indeed, installing an executive who acts like a CEO may be disastrous because a law firm cannot be run like other businesses. But equally disastrous is leaving too many decisions to the partnership vote. Individual partner actions (and more often nonaction) are driven by their own particular considerations and fears. This leads them to vote one way while acting another way. The result is a surreptitious corrosion of the firm, which is explained in more depth in Chapter 6, "Ecce Homo." The partnership itself is not a structure well-suited to leading. A chilling example that demonstrates this fact is Heller Ehrman.

The partnership itself is not a structure well-suited to leading

Heller Ehrman was founded in San Francisco in 1890 and, by 2006, had grown into an international law firm with more than 730 attorneys in 15 offices in the United States, Europe, and Asia. It had offices located in the key financial centers of New York; Los Angeles; Washington, DC; London; Beijing; Hong Kong; and Singapore. By all measures, Heller Ehrman was a healthy organization. It had organically grown to its peak size over time; there had been no blitz-expansion or exotic mergers. It did not have an egocentric leader, run costly media campaigns, or indulge in headline-making lateral trophy hunting. In 2007, the firm grossed $471 million with $1 million in profits per partner. A handful of partner departures had caused a decline in profits per partner by 3 percent that year, and Heller Ehrman had just entered merger talks with Mayer Brown. All of a sudden, a sizable group of 15 intellectual property litigators decamped to another firm. This was the ball of snow that started to accelerate down the mountain. The remaining partners became increasingly anxious. No one wanted to be the last lawyer left. Panic broke out. A total of 50 partners had left the firm in 2008, and Heller Ehrman dissolved. It was a classic run on the bank.

A firm of Heller Ehrman's size needs large clients, deals, and cases in order to sustain itself. Heller Ehrman successfully attracted these. A few departures by partners coincided with the closures of a number of large litigation cases and resulted in a down year. That is all. If you remember 2007, though, it was the boom time before the balloon burst. Insanely large mergers took place, clients spent lavishly, and law firms were thriving. In 2007, a drop by 3 percent in profit was enough for some partners to gripe about. Other firms were doing better. All of a sudden, the life of a business law firm seems very precarious.

Another victim of the snowball effect that results from partners leaving was Thelen. Formerly known as Thelen Reid Brown Raysman & Steiner, the firm had around 600 attorneys in 2006 with offices in eight cities in the United States, United Kingdom, and China. The firm was known for its construction practice, which dated back to the 1930s, having advised contractors and developers of large infrastructure projects, such as the Hoover Dam and the Golden Gate Bridge. It also offered legal advice concerning technology and outsourcing along with regulatory, transactional, and dispute resolution support. It further had eminent energy expertise, particularly in the electricity regulatory area. Thelen merged with Brown Raysman Millstein Felder & Steiner in 2006, creating a firm with revenues of over $400 million. But the two firms experienced trouble integrating with each other. The postmerger firm lost almost 200 attorneys between the merger and 2008, including many key partners and practice groups. In July 2008, the firm internally announced its intention to seek another merger partner. Merger discussions with East Coast firm Nixon Peabody failed, and between 60 and 90 attorneys went over to Nixon Peabody. In the autumn of 2008, the firm's partnership council recommended that the firm's partnership dissolve the firm.

Just like at Heller Ehrman, an initial relatively small drop in profit caused a wave of departing partners. The news release on its dissolution, issued by Thelen, contains the following passage:

> The decision to dissolve the firm was precipitated by several economic factors, including recessionary pressures and numerous partner departures over the past year, both of which have negatively impacted firm revenues. For the past several months, Thelen management has aggressively sought a full firm merger. Unfortunately, the most promising merger opportunity was derailed by conflicts, and all other full firm merger discussions terminated last week.
>
> The firm is in default of its primary credit agreement, having breached a partner departure covenant that restricts the number of partners who may depart the firm within any twelve-month period. As a result, the firm's bank now has control over expenditures.[8]

Every lawyer knows that large parts of the legal sector are inherently cyclical. As the economy unfolds through cycles of bull and bear markets, different practice areas burgeon and recede. Restructuring, insolvency, and litigation, for example, typically thrive in times when mergers and acquisitions suffer a drought. A larger law firm with diverse practice groups can even out some of the ups and downs. One year, the litigator may bring in a lot of business. The next year, it's the transactional lawyer. But Heller Ehrman, a more than century-old reputable firm, could not withstand even the slightest drop in profit. Thelen, whose legacy includes advising on some of the largest and most prestigious US infrastructure projects, suffered the same fate.

The final (2016) example is that of King & Wood Mallesons European arm. The firm started out as King & Wood PRC Lawyers, a high-ranked Chinese law firm, which in 2012 merged with Mallesons Stephen Jaques, one of the Big Six leading Australian law firms. In a move of bold expansion, King & Wood Mallesons shortly thereafter merged with UK-based international firm SJ Berwin, whose name disappeared into the new firm. SJ Berwin had, since the end of the 1990s, expanded throughout Europe and the Middle East. The firm was particularly well known for its market-leading investment funds practice having laid the legal foundations for private equity funds in the United Kingdom and Europe. Media repeatedly referred to SJ Berwin's partners as highly competitive and as part of silos rather than members of a one-firm team. The firm had a "famously tetchy partnership."[9] The financial crisis hit the private equity and real estate–related funds sector hard, and the firm suffered a near 50 percent drop in average PEP (profit per equity partner) from £800,000 in 2007 to £410,000 in 2008. SJ Berwin's leadership was looking to the United States for opportunities to grow out of its malaise, but none of the efforts came to fruition. Merger talks with New York's Proskauer Rose in 2010 failed in large part because of the disparity in profit levels. Capital contributions per partner at SJ Berwin were also less than half of most other firms, according to research done by *The American Lawyer*, which was a stumbling block for any merger.[10] In 2012, the firm decided to look east instead and engaged in merger talks with King & Wood Mallesons, and the merger went through in 2013, formed as a Swiss *verein*, an association of member organizations recognized under Swiss law. At the time, it was generally thought that SJ Berwin had traded down because of its top-tier legacy and reputation for client service. But even under its new name, the firm struggled to recuperate the profitability it had before 2008. It reported an anticipated drop in average PEP of roughly 10 percent for the 2012–2013 financial year. King & Wood Mallesons started a practice area restructuring near the end of 2015, and a 15 percent partner cut in the United Kingdom, Europe, and Middle East was announced at the beginning of 2016. From then on, the firm suffered an accelerating exodus of partners from its London headquarters. With SJ Berwin legacy partners described as cantankerous at best and money grubbing at worst, it was perhaps no wonder that there was little interest in "sticking it out" among London partners. Around 40 partners left the firm in Europe in 2016, including 24 whom the firm restructured out of the business. A recapitalization plan failed, with insufficient partners committing to the deal. By the end of 2016, the collapse of the European arm of King & Wood Mallesons was a fact.

Are the bonds between partners in today's law firms too weak to support even the slightest economic stress? The partner with a profitable practice in another office or in a different time zone may not be interested in carrying the load for a group of strangers who happen to be having a bad year. In today's legal landscape, are smaller partnerships perhaps more stable than larger ones despite their less stable turnover? I would say that, even though partner mobility has increased exponentially in some markets and is an important contributing factor to why business law firms might collapse, the answer is more complex than partner stability and slight financial fluctuations. Chapter by chapter in this book, the pieces of the puzzle that make up the business of law firms will show that it is far from a simple picture.

Two extremes have been clearly represented in the failing firms of the first decade. At one end of the spectrum, we find the firm driven blindly by greed with a charismatic leader at the helm. At the other end of the spectrum is the firm with a lack of vision and leadership, leaving the partnership as the only structure by which the firm functions. As pernicious as a lack of governance is, a lack of ambition is equally dangerous. These days, partnerships are only as strong as last year's profit.

Looking ahead, running a law firm will be even more challenging. Having witnessed some of these collapses close up and observed the inner workings of law firms for 20 years, I can predict with confidence that over 30 percent of all business-oriented law firms are at risk of collapse. At this very moment, one after another of the best partners are bleeding away from well-established business law firms. This peril exists irrespective of which market a law firm is in, although I dare say that it will be more prominent in the midmarket segment. In order to elaborate further, we first need to paint a picture of the array of markets in which law firms operate.

KEY POINTS

- Law firms are not immune to failure: history has proven that law firms do collapse, even the ones that are perceived as being among the most successful.

- The collapse is sudden, unexpected, and fast. Nobody sees it coming.
- Drivers for failure have been, in various combinations,
  - drop in profit: even a slight drop can cause a run on the bank;
  - fast geographical expansion and rapid increase in partner headcount;
  - fixed costs that are too high;
  - overly adventurous partner compensation models; and
  - lack of governance.

2

IT'S NOT LIKE IT USED TO BE

Over the past two decades, the global legal market has changed significantly. Law firms have expanded considerably outside their home jurisdictions. Some of them have followed their core clients as they have grown into international corporate or financial institutions. Others have aimed to secure the cross-border work generated by international clients, winning market share from local firms that lack an international brand. At the same time, strong national firms seem to thrive with a higher turnover than ever. There is, however, a clear pattern as to how the segmentation of the legal market will look in the coming decade.

The very top segment of the global legal market is dominated by the Global Elite firms, a small group of firms that get called in for bet-the-farm matters of the *Fortune* Global 500 companies as well as mega-transactions and initial public offerings (IPOs) where money is no object. Bordering on the Global Elite we find other nonglobalized top-tier US law firms, predominantly based in New York, as well as the London Magic Circle. This segment occasionally picks a deal from the Global Elite but generally handles similar matters, also servicing the *Fortune* Global 500 companies but on a slightly smaller scale. The midmarket segment is led by the international business law

(IBL) firms together with strong national champions, the large independent national law firms, that focus on upper midtier work with the occasional large deal. Beneath that, we find the midmarket firms that are typically involved in a high volume of a client's standard business operations on a local level and, beneath that, the firms that efficiently perform commodity bulk work at competitive prices.

The members of the Global Elite have carved out a niche for themselves in which they virtually monopolize all the international mega-transactions. The longstanding relationships of several Wall Street law firms with investment and commercial banking clients have made these firms emerge as preeminent among business law firms. When a bet-the-farm matter comes along anywhere globally, it is given to only a handful of firms, such as Skadden, Sullivan & Cromwell, Wachtell Lipton, Cravath, Simpson Thatcher, Weil Gotshal, Davis Polk, or Cleary Gottlieb. The leading Wall Street firms started competing in the European market during the late 1990s; however, they had established their presence decades earlier through representative offices practicing only US law. The large industrial and economic restructuring of Europe that took place in the 1990s invited the Wall Street law firms to the party because they had expertise and competence that the European firms lacked. Ever since then, they have remained focused on the very high-end segment of the legal market in Europe, as well as globally, to the extent that they have established a near monopoly. Mergermarket's 2016 league table of the top 10 law firms advising on mergers and acquisitions in Europe,[1] ranked by deal value, is almost entirely dominated by Global Elite and Magic Circle firms. On June 1, 2015, the front-page headline of the *Financial Times* read, "US Dealmaking Hits $243bn Monthly Record"[2] The month of May 2015 had been the biggest M&A month ever in US-bound deals—with an incredible $243 billion—surpassing records set in the debt and dot-com booms of 2007 and 2000, respectively; 2016 was the runner-up record year since 2007. This number is mainly attributable to a handful of very large deals. Looking at the law firms involved, the earnings of this M&A boom stay within the Global Elite. Many of these firms do not even have a significant office in the jurisdiction that they dominate. They tend to be present only in international financial centers because their matters are largely financially driven, and their dominant expertise in capital markets is key. The firms that belong to today's Global Elite all have a strong US base. This is presumably why the Magic Circle firms are running just one step behind; none of them have a significant presence in the United States, whereas the Global Elite tend to have a strong presence in the United Kingdom.

The members of the Global Elite have carved out a niche for themselves in which they virtually monopolize all international mega-transactions

According to *The American Lawyer* Global 100 overview,[3] based on the numbers of 2015–16 financial year, there are 35 law firms with a turnover above $1 billion, and 10 of those have a turnover of more than $2 billion. The global legal services market is estimated to have a total turnover of up to $660 billion in 2016.[4] TheCityUK's UK Legal Services 2016[5] report estimates the global legal market to be worth around $618 billion in 2014–15. Assuming the total turnover is $650 billion, the top 10 law firms together represent 3.5 percent of that market, and the top 35 represent 8.5 percent. Although the total turnover of the legal services market is small in comparison to other markets, one could conclude that there is still room to compete. It is not a shrinking market. Just looking at the US market, even though the total number of billable hours by law firms largely remained flat the last six years,[6] the legal work that clients generate has been increasing.[7]

The three highest-grossing law firms of *The American Lawyer* Global 100 overview are not Global Elite or Magic Circle firms: they are IBL firms. The emerging IBL firms have seen an opportunity to compete for cross-border work outside the competitive scope of corporate transactions. They handle midmarket to upper midmarket transactions as well as litigation, real estate, and higher-value commercial work. This category is in transition and is spread out over several segments of the legal market. Examples of IBL firms that are competing in the upper segments of the legal market are Latham & Watkins and Mayer Brown. There is also a group of IBL firms that has emerged as Goliaths and are continuing to build in size. These firms are determined to be present wherever their current and future clients may do business. In 2012, SNR Denton unveiled its union with French firm Salans and Canadian outfit Fraser Milner Casgrain to become Dentons. In 2015, Dentons announced a merger with China's largest law firm, Dacheng, vaulting the firm from 2,368 lawyers to about 6,400 with an instant presence throughout China. It has since announced mergers that will take it into the United States and further into Asia. Squire Sanders and Hogan Lovells have also undergone transatlantic mergers to take their present form. US law firm Squire, Sanders & Dempsey and the British firm of Hammonds formed a sizable firm with 1,275 lawyers in 37 offices and 17 countries through their merger in the beginning of 2011. Norton Rose has likewise opened in Australia, South Africa, and Canada on the back of three mergers with local firms. DLA Piper, being the largest law firm in the world based on turnover, is continuing to build its position globally through mergers and exclusive alliances. The list goes on.

A growing number of IBL firms are incorporated as Swiss vereins, which gives them flexibility to vary their compensation structure per market. The fast-expanding firms mentioned previously—Dentons, Squire Sanders, Hogan Lovells, Norton Rose, and DLA Piper, as well as Baker & McKenzie—are all incorporated as Swiss vereins. Baker & McKenzie was the first major law firm to become a Swiss verein, in 2004. Swiss vereins were originally designed for the (international) affiliation of nonprofit entities, sports clubs, or unions. Amnesty International, the World Wildlife Fund (WWF), and the Fédération Internationale de Football Association (FIFA), to name a few, are all Swiss vereins.

A Swiss verein law firm is formed through articles of association without creating an entity that actually practices law. Instead, the member law firms independently render legal services and severally accept the liabilities that accompany such work. Thus, members do not share commercial or professional liability for the debts or actions of other member firms. They also do not share the profits. The articles of association must be written and approved by at least two persons who will function as officers in the company. A governing board, such as a board of directors, must be elected, with each elected official meeting the requirements set forth in Swiss law. Auditors who will monitor the financial dealings of the organization must also be identified.

A Swiss verein allows a collection of law firms, organized under different corporate or partnership structures in different countries, to present themselves internationally under a single brand without having to comply with the regulations and tax codes of each other's countries. This arrangement conveniently avoids potential restrictive bar association regulations and complicated tax reporting. As a result, it is the ideal form for law firms that aim to take on large mergers. But not sharing profit also removes the very incentive for partners to share clients and work between the member partnerships. Critics argue that merged partners who continue to operate independently after the merger are in effect only a marketing platform.

Interestingly, being incorporated as a Swiss verein has been used as a defense argument in cases on conflict of interest. Dentons argued in May 2015, before the US International Trade Commission, that the Swiss verein structure essentially established an "ethical screen" between its Canadian and US entities. Dentons US LLP was set to represent RevoLaze LLC in a patent suit against Gap Inc. Gap filed the motion to disqualify Dentons, arguing that Gap had long been a client of Dentons Canada, which placed the firm in a conflict of interest. Judge Charles Bullock rejected Dentons's argument that the Swiss verein structure would in any way be an argument against conflict of interest: "Dentons holds itself out to the public as a unified global law firm in order to attract business, and Dentons' continued representation in the face of a direct conflict would both contradict this public image and negatively impact the law profession as a whole."[8]

Swiss verein law firms have argued that member firms do not share privileged information with other member firms unless they are retained by and working together for a client on the same matter. The decision by the US International Trade Commission on Dentons representing Gap, however, may give them pause for thought. Another concern when it comes to "file sharing" is the one connected to the large international firms that have formed through mergers involving Chinese law firms. Western corporate clients are not comfortable with their files being potentially accessible by law firms who are still Chinese firms despite operating under an international name. Whether or not such concerns are justified is beyond the scope of this book; however, it may be another stumbling block for the Swiss vereins that have entered China.

Other international firms, such as Herbert Smith Freehills and Ashurst, both UK firms, have expanded through mergers while keeping a more traditional profit-sharing structure in place. Another thing that most IBL firms have in common is that they originate in the United States or have a dominant US part. This commonality exists not only because large and medium cross-border transactions are done under US law and businesses everywhere turn to US capital markets to raise funds but also because the global legal market is affected by the extraterritoriality of US law. A country of such economic power that claims so much extraterritorial jurisdiction creates a need for US legal advice nearly anywhere globally.

In markets where the international firms have strengthened their local capabilities, the national firms are often left with lower-value local work

The national champions are increasingly disadvantaged in the larger corporate and institutional market. The international firms bring a number of competitive advantages that a national firm finds hard to replicate, such as cross-border capabilities, international reputation and brand, and significant resources both in branding and support to fee earners, including the use of legal process outsourcing and advanced technology. In markets where the international firms have strengthened their local capabilities, the national firms are often left with lower-value local work. National law firms are faced with the choice of opening supporting offices in other jurisdictions to facilitate transactions across time zones and cultures or to enter some form of alliance. Having a supporting office outside of the firm's jurisdiction is often unprofitable. The lawyers are paid on expat terms, often including an allowance for the expatriation of the whole family. The partners who are sent out to a satellite office rarely have a workload that requires them to maintain full speed, not to mention the considerably lower leverage they can maintain. Choosing to recruit locally is a risk, diluting the strength of the partnership, as was made clear in many of the stories of the failed law firms presented in Chapter 1, "Icarus's Fall." An office abroad also means taking on currency risk as well as coping with the differences in liabilities across different jurisdictions. The level of the billing rates also fluctuates across jurisdictions and markets. Local firms experience this effect through the inflated rates often carried by an international deal. Having said all this, there may still be convincing reasons to open an office abroad. The most notable scramble to open an office in recent years has been focused on China. To date, the vast majority of foreign law firms' offices in China are not profitable. Yet, a case can be made for some of them that a foot on the ground there is very helpful.

ALLIANCES

Some top-tier national law firms seek their solution to the dilemma of whether to have an international presence in some form of alliance with national champions in other jurisdictions. Even one Magic Circle firm chose to operate with an alliance. London-based Slaughter and May relies on referral relationships with its "best friends" for nearly all of its international work. A *best friend network* is an international club formed by a handful of law firms in different countries where the members will refer matters almost exclusively to each other. Linklaters also forged alliances in Australia and South Africa in 2012. Exclusive alliances have been characterized as an uneasy compromise between a full merger and a loose referral arrangement. An alliance may be a loose confederation of separate offices or practices, but it is meant to bring the client the benefit of one engagement letter, one lead partner, and one invoice. It may be a preferred way to compete against the international firms' dominance while bringing what many clients are looking for: local expertise in every jurisdiction.

Another group of top 20 European firms teamed up in 2012 based on that idea: Italy's Chiomenti Studio Legale, Spanish firm Cuatrecasas Gonçalves Pereira, France's Gide Loyrette Nouel, and German firm Gleiss Lutz. In 2014, a so-called customized alliance made headlines, designed to fulfill the wishes of a single client with a global brand: the Nike Alliance. The Customized Alliance for Nike is a purpose-built one-stop shop consisting of 21 firms covering 17 jurisdictions, all working for Nike. They have all agreed to offer a flat-fee rate to Nike across the jurisdictions, as well as consistent working procedures. Each jurisdiction has a firm that fits Nike's needs. The alliance was initiated by Kennedy van der Laan, a Dutch national midtier firm with a focus on information technology (IT) and intellectual property. The alliance is managed from Amsterdam by a dedicated team, and the firms regularly get together to share information and best practices. Nike is not the first company to go down this route. Construction support services giant Carillion has operated a "Carillion network" for a number of years, asking its panel of firms to operate collaboratively in a bid to improve efficiency.

MERGERS AND SPINOFFS

Beyond the IBL firms are a number of expanding law firms that do not entirely fit the mentioned molds. These are firms that have chosen to merge for instant presence in one or two more major markets without entering the category of the IBL firms. In 2011, London-based Ashurst announced its merger with Australian firm Blake Dawson and instantly gained a foothold in Hong Kong, Singapore, Tokyo, Shanghai, and Jakarta. Australia can be an appealing market for law firms looking to expand because of the country's trading ties with China, along with a wealth of natural resources. Likewise, in 2012, the United Kingdom's Herbert Smith and Australia's Freehills voted to combine after Herbert Smith saw its alliance with Gleiss Lutz (Germany) and Stibbe (Netherlands) fall apart due to those firms' unwillingness to merge. The merger between King & Wood in China with Mallesons Stephen Jaques in Australia and SJ Berwin in Europe formed the first and only global law firm based out of Asia and the largest law firm headquartered outside of the United States or European Union, at least until the European arm collapsed at the end of 2016.

Similar to the IBL firms, other firms have scrambled to put together an international footprint in order to stay competitive. In 2016, law firms Olswang, Nabarro, and CMS UK agreed to merge. The new entity will have more than 1,000 partners and a global revenue of more than €1.2 billion. That same year, Eversheds finally found US coverage in law firm Sutherland Asbill & Brennan. The combined Eversheds Sutherland will have 2,300 lawyers and 61 offices in 29 countries. Many more firms have had cross-continental merger talks that have come far before failing, and they are continuing to search.

Looking at the intra-European market, mergers are relatively rare, although lately firms have made efforts to enter Germany, perhaps in a bid to position themselves for a market after Brexit. Except for this, there is little need for any law firm to establish a bigger presence in any single European country. The individual markets do not represent sufficient opportunities for growth. Furthermore, there is not enough cross-border workflow between European countries to warrant a cross-border merger of law firms. No client is asking for such a development. Instead, the trend toward groups of partners leaving to form boutique businesses continues expeditiously. Most commonly, this trend is due to law firms shedding partners in practice areas that no longer fit the firm's focus. These partners feel undervalued and leave their firms to form boutique outfits with top-quality advice offered at competitive rates because they do not have the same cost structure as the full service firms. This trend started in the area of intellectual property and IT about a decade ago, but since then, other areas have emerged, including boutique M&A firms that are highly profitable. The new type of high-end boutique firm is formed by partners from core practice areas of first-tier firms that see an opportunity to offer clients flexibility at competitive prices because of their lower cost base. In France, for example, during the past three years, the emergence of the boutique firms has been pronounced. Darrois Villey Maillot Brochier, Gide Loyrette Nouel, Hogan Lovells, and Sullivan & Cromwell all said adieu to partners in Paris as they set off on their own. The same development has been confirmed to take place in Germany. TGO Consulting's report on partner mobility in the German market showed that 14 high-end corporate/M&A boutiques had been formed in the past five years, all by equity partners from the top 25 firms.[9] This is serious new competition for top-tier law firms who used to count high-value mergers and acquisitions as their exclusive territory.

At the same time that law firms merge or break up in the ever-shifting legal market, the lateral movement of individual partners has become more frequent. Nearly every week there is an update on lateral moves between competing firms. In 2016, a star partner from Cravath—thought to be the last bastion of the true partnership—left for Paul Weiss. Before this, only a very few partners, counted on one hand, had ever moved to competing firms. Cravath operates a pure lockstep system, whereas Paul Weiss and other firms like it tend to link remuneration more with performance. In London, we have in recent years witnessed a war for talent between US and Magic Circle firms, which have sent the latter scrambling to review their rigid lockstep system that prevents lucrative signing fees or other incentives that lure rainmakers. The Magic Circle firms often argue that lockstep directly incentivizes partners to cooperate for the greater good of the firm. But lockstep is also arguably a weakness when it comes to attracting and retaining top partner talent. In the US market, there were 2,890 lateral moves at the top 200 law firms in the financial year 2015, according to *The American Lawyer*.[10] In 2001, that number was 1,998, which means that the past decade has seen an increase in partner mobility of nearly 70 percent. This trend will not subside. Once a partner makes that move, there is nothing but attractive work and profit that will make him or her stay put. A survey conducted by Motive Legal Consulting, encompassing 2,869 lateral partner moves in London from January 1, 2006, to December 31, 2013, concluded that nearly a third of the laterally hired partners had moved on again.[11] This finding suggests that once a partner starts moving, it is likely that he or she will move again.

NETWORKS

The international networks that give members access to other jurisdictions on a nonexclusive basis are at the loose end of alliance structures. There are numerous international networks. Chambers and Partners lists 10 of them as the global elite of networks: First Law International, Interlaw, Interlex Group, Lex Mundi, Meritas, Multilaw, PRAC, TAGLaw, TerraLex, World Law Group, and World Services Group. A law firm network may not be essential to the members' strategy, but it offers valuable opportunistic elements. Founded in 1989, Lex Mundi is a premier network of law firms with a global membership of 160 firms, including firms working in less common jurisdictions where it might be difficult to find a reliable partner. Lex Mundi has one member from the upper tiers of each jurisdiction. There is a rigorous procedure to be permitted into the network, and periodic membership reviews ensure all members keep up the quality of their work and service levels. For example, in recent years, the need for African presence has become more pressing, and a network such as Lex Mundi offers instant access to 17 law firms throughout the continent, which have been subjected to the same scrutiny as all other members.

The most successful networks know that a personal relationship between referring firms and partners is key for the trust that is needed for serious referrals. They have a structure in place to ensure multiple face-to-face meeting opportunities between members every year. Networks like these can give national law firms the international reach that they need. Convincing the client of the value of the network, however, is often a matter of marketing the individual firm on a pitch-by-pitch basis. Many networks have a marketing or business development outfit of their own, but it is a hard battle to coordinate and convince a group of strong and independent firms to cobrand. The true weak point of a network stems from another factor: at the larger law firms, a network membership is typically used as a reward for a senior partner who in the past has done great service to the firm. Each member firm has a contact partner who represents the firm at annual network gatherings and conferences. The contact partners get to fly all over the world to events hosted by top-tier law firms that will do their utmost to be the most generous of hosts. Expenses are rarely spared. The contact partner is also often the first to receive referrals from a member in the network, which contributes to keeping the practice of the contact partner running. The problem with this system is that these contact partners tend to be lone wolves and are rarely able to have enough sway in their own partnership to be able to implement the promises made by the network. Referrals and joint pitching, the raison d'être of an international network, have to be done on a broad front within the law firms, but to many partners the network might be largely unknown. Referrals are based on trust between individual partners. This organizational flaw says nothing about the quality of the network, but it does mean that it has unused potential. Networks are rarely anchored properly within the member firms of the largest jurisdictions.

ACCOUNTANTS AND ALTERNATIVE SERVICE PROVIDERS

In an overview of the current legal market and what this may look like in the coming decade, there is no way around the Big Four accountants: PwC (formerly PricewaterhouseCoopers), Deloitte Touche Tohmatsu, EY (formerly Ernst & Young), and KPMG (Klynveld Peat Marwick Goerdeler). Recently, they have reiterated their ambition to establish a global legal services arm, which will offer many of the business-as-usual services their clients require. It is a development that should be taken seriously simply because of the standing of the Big Four and their level of penetration with clients. The large accountants' previous attempt to capture a share of the legal market was halted when the Enron scandal brought down Andersen. Accountants had to move away from bundling services and sold off their nontax legal branches. But with the turmoil in the legal market after 2008, the Big Four started to see renewed opportunities and have recently begun to move fast.

The Economist[12] reported in March 2015 that the combined annual revenues of the Big Four's accounting networks, $120 billion, exceed the $89 billion generated by the 100 largest law firms combined. This revenue provides them with impressive fire power. In 2014, EY announced that it had recruited a Freshfields partner, Richard Norbruis, to handle the global expansion of its law practice. EY launched legal services in 29 countries around the world, including Australia, China, Japan, Mexico, and 14 separate countries in Africa. Its legal services cover transactional, commercial, and employment practices, with a strong focus on the financial services and banking industries.

The same year, the head of PwC's legal arm (PwC Legal) announced the firm's ambition to become a global top 20 legal services player within the next five years. It told *The Lawyer* that "the firm was targeting revenues of $1 billion—doubling from 2013's almost $500m across the firm's legal offering—with particular growth earmarked for Asia and Africa." In the United Kingdom, the Legal Services Act 2007 came into effect in 2011, allowing nonlawyers in professional, management, or ownership roles to offer regulated legal services in England and Wales. PwC has, under the Legal Services Act, been granted an alternative business structure license in order to provide legal services to clients. By the end of 2016, PwC Legal revenues had grown by more than 40 percent over the previous two financial years. Deloitte is on the same path with Deloitte Legal. "Deloitte is focused on creating the premier global law firm, with the goal of realizing independent legal practices in over 100 countries by 2020," a spokesman of Deloitte has told the legal press.[13] The firm has claimed to have a continuing six-year streak of double-digit growth of its legal arm.

The ambition of the Big Four is a force to be reckoned with. They have the client contacts, and unlike law firms, they do not have an information gap regarding clients' operations and are armed with operational excellence. Accounting firms are prevented from owning law firms in the United States, Brazil, and India, but they are allowed to own law firms in Britain, Australia, and Mexico and, through collaboration and cost sharing, can offer legal services in jurisdictions such as France, Germany, Spain, Italy, Japan, and China. This gives the Big Four an advantage over international law firms in the enormous growth market of China. For some reason, Chinese regulations allow international accounting firms, but not international law firms, to offer domestic legal services in China. Western accounting firms have expanded extensively in China through the acquisition of Chinese accounting firms. The Big Four accounting firms have enjoyed a dominant position in China's accounting and auditing industry for decades without many restrictions. By expanding into legal advisory work, they aim to build on the amount of work they are already doing for top Chinese companies. In such an emerging market, they may be able to catch more high-value legal work than they have been able to catch so far in the western markets.

Beyond the Big Four, in-house counsel have access to a new breed of service providers that allow them flexibility in response to an ever-changing flow of work. Even before the financial crisis, a new type of company was honing in on that perfect combination of legal expertise and the business processes and tools of the Big Four. Since then, alternative legal service providers have come a long way from merely offering flexible workforce and high-volume/low-value tasks, such as document review. Client demand and funding from large investors have caused this sector to develop with incredible speed. If today's alternative service providers were inventoried here, the sector would already have moved to the next-generation service providers by the time you read this book.

Alternative service providers started by offering secondments and interim workforce—all alumni of the best law firms and companies—to in-house legal departments. They have since evolved to provide large clients with tailor-made, technology-driven solutions for—sometimes complex—bulk work. Their teams include technologists, process engineers, management consultants, and expert lawyers set on delivering not just legal advice but entire solutions for any client's largest area of inside spend. Few of these providers use the billable hour because it does not make sense to price solutions aided by technology in increments of time. Instead, they offer subscriptions or fixed-rate contracts, which gives clients the benefit of being able to predict and control their budget. However, it is important to put this sector into perspective. Media might report that one alternative service provider is more successful than another, but looking at the current market share of alternative service providers in the United States, it is estimated they represent only $1 billion of the $437 billion legal market.[14]

Changes to the rules that define the legal market will continue to occur. The United Kingdom's Legal Services Act was just a start: many other jurisdictions are looking over their rules to respond to the same regulatory objectives to remove restrictions to competition and improve access to justice. The Legal Services Act undeniably introduced the atmosphere of liberalization in the UK market and opened possibilities that are attractive to entrepreneurial thinkers and new market entrants. In the past few years, there also has been an increasing debate about whether legal privilege should apply to transactional lawyers. An M&A lawyer is part of a transactional team in a corporate acquisition in the same way as the financial advisors, tax advisors, and accountants.

Why should the advice provided by the lawyer be legally protected while the advice of the others is not? Legal privilege has been put in place to ensure an open and unrestricted conversation between client and lawyer without fear that it may be used against the client in a court of law. Such a privilege may have no obvious place in business acquisitions. The privilege of legal privilege might soon be a thing of the past, and corporate transaction lawyers will again find themselves in a changed market.

CHANGES ON CLIENT SIDE

Since 2008, clients—driven to a large extent by an economic imperative to bring down the overall costs of legal services—started to take control of key decisions. Clients with a global presence have in the past few years been weeding out their law firm panels because they were no longer corresponding to their needs. Year after year, surveys conclude that demand for law firm services has stagnated. At the same time, the legal services needs of companies have grown. An increasing share of companies' legal work tends to be done in-house. The position of the in-house lawyer has undergone a transformation in the past decade. Before the global financial crisis struck, most general counsel were more concerned with the quality of services than the price of them. These days, general counsel are almost without exception pressured by budget cuts and looking more closely at the value–price relation. Another change that has occurred in comparison to precrisis practices is that general counsel more frequently have a seat at the board and are participating on a daily basis in the strategic decision making of the company.

Over the nine past years, I have been involved in an annual research into the evolving role of the in-house lawyer. A notable change that happened right before our eyes during those nine years is how in-house legal departments have been increasing in size and quality. They now more often than not contain young, smart, and very ambitious lawyers. In-house legal departments in successful companies are streamlined, efficient, and highly talented. Half of the in-house lawyers in an international company typically have many years' experience in a law firm. National law firms that have been unwilling to change or expand their partnership structure have created an excess talent pool of young, smart lawyers who have been snapped up by growing international companies. A good friend of mine, a former partner of a top-tier law firm, was brought in to set up an in-house litigation department for a large international insurance group. This litigation unit now works as a purpose-built law firm with its offices inside the walls of its one client.

The in-house lawyers we came across during our research not only are smart and ambitious but also have unparalleled sector knowledge, an attuned business sense, and a consistently practical approach. These in-house lawyers have come to expect that the panel law firms they work with for external advice will have to be clued in on their business—a smaller panel will foster a closer relationship—and will have to offer a seamless international reach.

Looking at the spread of the *Fortune* Global 500 companies between 2000 and today, they have gone from being located primarily in the United States and European Union to being spread across the globe. They have also come to expect more of their panel firms. In a large company, the legal department is regularly assisted by procurement professionals who handle the process of panel appointments. They have cost and efficiency targets with objective measurements that apply equally to all bidders. They have a clear role within the company that in some cases not even the preferences of the legal department can override. Often, requests for proposals require value-added services, such as secondments and access to information systems and templates. These costs are more easily absorbed by an IBL firm, while it might be a real burden for a much smaller national law firm.

The procurement department charged with appointing a panel of law firms will go for the best package deal even if this means a small compromise on quality in one or two jurisdictions. This new type of international client has provided the IBL firms with an advantage, at the expense of the national law firm. Indeed, the cost of sales has dramatically increased for a law firm. It must invest more nonchargeable time into obtaining and maintaining a client relationship.

It used to be that in-house legal departments had a bad reputation. They were seen as stumbling blocks within companies—the department of No. The commercial people felt that if you handed anything to Legal, it would take weeks before they responded, and then they would only give you reasons why something could not be done. This reputation developed because in-house lawyers acted the same as lawyers in general: covering their asses. Reasons for not giving a straight answer could have included the possibility of being wrong, not wanting the responsibility, and in general having difficulty evaluating options in a descending order from *preferable* to *not recommended.* This hesitancy to commit to a definitive answer has changed. The boards and leadership of large companies decided to alter the parameters. First, the legal department had to start working more as a team and become integrated in the business process. Second, and most crucial, companies started to recognize the concept of *risk appetite.* A company operates and makes decisions regarding the future in accordance with its risk appetite. Different companies have different risk appetites, but every organization has one whether it acknowledges it explicitly or not. It is the mutual understanding between executive management and the board regarding the drivers of, and parameters around, opportunity-seeking behavior. The in-house lawyers have to get on board and and align their strategies with the company's guidelines. When looking into a possible way forward, members of the legal department will have to quantify the risk on the one hand and the gains on the other. The particular risk appetite of their company tells them how much risk they can accept in return for potential gains and leads them to answer the board accordingly with a recommendation.

I was once responsible for the commercial activities of an international retail chain. The board came to me and said that all competitors used a form of lottery as a marketing tool in one of their main markets, and could we not do the same? Holding a lottery, or a game of chance, without a gambling license was forbidden in this particular jurisdiction. The competitors were trying to circumvent these rules by choosing the winners among customers beforehand and then asking all customers to participate. I referred the question to our external lawyer and received back the uninspired conclusion that there was legislation in force that forbade this kind of game of chance. The answer I *wanted* to receive was: "Although there is indeed a law that technically forbids this kind of lottery, it is considered outdated and is no longer enforced. If you do go ahead and use this promotional tool, ensure that the gains exceed the potential fine of $25,000."

Lawyers in a law firm work as a consequence of an external stimulus: they act when asked to by their client. They wait for an instruction. Working in a law firm is a reactive occupation. The lawyers who want to make the switch to become an in-house counsel will have to switch to a more proactive stance. In a law firm, there is no board that imposes a different way of working. There is no concept of risk appetite for a law firm. If there were, the risk appetite would be zero. The core of their contribution to the process is that they are asked to look at an issue and give an opinion. In a sense, they are constantly asked to give a guarantee as to whether or not a certain action can be taken. Lawyers face serious consequences if they are wrong. This risk leads them to be cautious. Therefore, clients do not always receive the kind of advice they want. Clients are not looking for zero risk; they are looking for a weighing of risks that answers the question, *Does it make business sense?* This disparity between the needs of corporate clients and the risk aversity of law firm advisors seems hard to bridge.

There is no concept of risk appetite for a law firm. If there were, the risk appetite would be zero

THE IT REVOLUTION

Regularly, IT has been announced as the dead ringer for the traditional law firm. The days of using interns to plough through a massive number of documents at relatively low but profitable rates are quickly disappearing. Automation and smart software have changed the due diligence and discovery procedures and have already started to take over many tasks performed by law firm trainees, professional support lawyers, and junior associates. Software programs can perform data-related tasks more precisely, more quickly, and in greater volumes than a human can. Today's applications are somewhat limited in meeting the needs of a busy firm, but development is ongoing and the software capabilities improve with each iteration.

The computer debate for lawyers arguably started with Watson. The artificially intelligent computer system developed by IBM was catapulted to fame in 2011 by winning the television quiz show *Jeopardy!* in competition against humans. This event might have gone unnoticed in the legal market had not the general counsel of IBM at that time suggested that Watson might be used for legal research. This generated a flood of speculation among lawyers that has not stopped since. Watson is not a single entity but rather a developer cloud, which IBM has made available in different applications that other developers can use to build on. This artificially intelligent system can answer questions posed in natural language and uses multiple algorithms simultaneously to come to a probable answer. A number of applications are already on the market and are used by law firms as assistants on the level of support lawyers or junior associates. But it is nonsense to say that artificial intelligence will ever replace lawyers. Artificially intelligent systems are not designed to make decisions or to replace the senior lawyer. Yet many people persist in believing so.

In 2013, two economists at the University of Oxford Martin Programme on the Impacts of Future Technology conducted a study to estimate the future impact of computerization on the US labor market.[15] The study, prompted by the many cognitive tasks that are computerized owing to the availability of big data, examines what parameters have an impact on the likelihood of computerization and looks into more than 700 types of jobs to categorize them according to levels of probability. Jobs requiring perception and manipulation, creativity, and social intelligence were identified as those least likely to be computerized. Jobs that involve consulting other people, negotiating agreements, resolving problems, and coordinating activities require a great deal of social intelligence, which computers are unlikely to take over. "Most management, business, and finance occupations, which are intensive in generalist tasks requiring social intelligence, are largely confined to the low risk category," the study says.[16]

Washington Post graphics editor Shelly Tan designed an interactive graphic,[17] based on the University of Oxford study, that predicts the likelihood of various occupations being overtaken by computers. The probability of a robot replacing a lawyer is a low 3.46 percent. Paralegals and legal assistants, on the other hand, didn't do so well, with a probability of 94.46 percent that their jobs will be computerized because their work is simply more routine. Even so, the topic of computers replacing lawyers in the legal world lingers.

The true IT revolution will always be around the corner, and the notion of computers replacing lawyers will never quite be discredited. In the meantime, the media, wrongly assuming that the legal profession consists of antediluvian, backwards-looking people, will forever present it with a tone of doom. Technology is not the great disruptor. It will not be the cause of the end of lawyers, nor the demise of law firms. Instead, it is part of the answer to the question of what will help them survive.

Technology is not the great disruptor. Instead, it will be part of the answer

The single-most influential factor on the business models of law firms is commoditization of the legal market. Using technology, along with a changed business model, will be the only effective response for many law firms. The developments during 2016 in legal funding show how commodity legal work can become a cash cow with the help of technology. Low- or medium-value litigation has long been commoditized legal work. Together with algorithms and predictive analysis technology, such litigation has entered a new phase. Third-party investors have for quite some time in many jurisdictions been able to fund a lawsuit in return for a cut of the reward. But now, based on historical lawsuit data, software can predict the chances for success of a lawsuit. Along with other data, such as the type of case, legal merits, and level of solvency of the defendant, the managed risk and return on investment becomes very attractive for an investor. Some see this as a tool of greed, others as access to justice. Either way, it shows how well technology can enable new solutions for what was left behind as a dying business.

The single-most influential factor on the business models of law firms is commoditization of the legal market

KEY POINTS

- Top of the market transactional work and bet-the-farm matters are almost monopolized by the Global Elite.

- An ever-growing category of midmarket global law firms has emerged, and they are now taking an increasing part of the market in almost every jurisdiction.
- On a national level, newly formed small boutique firms, with lower costs, are getting mandates from clients and have become serious competition for the incumbent firms.
- New competitors, such as the Big Four accounting firms and alternative business structures, are slowly but surely eating their way into the legal market.
- In-house legal departments are better equipped, staffed, and organized than ever before. Downward pressure on the cost of outside legal counsel remains strong and will increase.
- Intelligent computer software has matured over the past decade and is now capable of carrying out tasks performed by trainees, junior lawyers, and paralegals. This evolution undermines the business model.

3

WORLDS APART

To fully appreciate the dynamics of the legal landscape, it is important to briefly sketch a map of the global legal market. It would be overly ambitious to deliver a thorough and complete description of the legal market in each jurisdiction in one chapter, or even in one book. This chapter provides a brief sketch of the legal market in some jurisdictions with the objective of illustrating that the scene is complex. Although law firms are sufficiently alike to warrant generalization to a certain extent, each law firm is formed against the background of particular cultural and historical circumstances and operates in different markets. This makes each and every law firm unique, something that is seldom sufficiently taken into account when trying to find a tonic for any ailing financial results or attempting to devise a strategy for the future.

There is one main driver shaping the legal markets of individual countries: its clients. Their size, number, and international orientation dictate the mix of national and international law firms. How companies are shaped and how they operate determines the configuration of the law firms they use. How the economy is faring and the total size of the market determine how many larger law firms can be sustained.

Today, international capability is viewed by many as inherent to the practice of business law as law firms increasingly grow to serve the needs of their global business clients. Becoming international or global is not necessarily appropriate for every law firm, though. A large number of law firms have a presence in a variety of countries around the world, but this does not mean that they have necessarily invested wisely. Any law firm with two or more offices in different countries can be characterized as international. But for many of the firms with an office in London, New York, Shanghai, and Brussels, the office's primary purpose is to be paraded on their website. Only six firms of the Global 100[1] are located in only one country. The other firms together have offices on every continent except Antarctica.

For many law firms with an office in London, New York, Shanghai, and Brussels, the office's primary purpose is to be paraded on their website

A second factor that contributes to shaping legal markets is the history of a jurisdiction, which determines language and legal system. The presence of Portuguese law firms in Lusophone Africa, for example, is not entirely attributable to having followed their clients into this region. They may simply practice there because they can. Sheer economic force has helped common law and the English language to dominate major corporate transactions internationally, but this was certainly facilitated by the fact that the English language and common law were spread across the world through historical geopolitics, trade, and colonialism. Spanish firms, likewise, have a significant presence in Latin America, while French firms can be found in Francophone Africa, Indochina, and other former colonies or historical trade partners. A country that is by culture more nationalistic will predominantly have clients that are biased toward their own culture and language. Such a market will be dominated by local law firms with a conservative structure. In countries where clients are "open," national law firms at the top end of the market cannot survive without an international network. The market itself can be closed off to foreign law firms in a form of protectionism. For example, it is virtually impossible for a foreigner to practice Indian law, although in July 2015, the Indian Supreme Court ruled that foreign lawyers who wish to practice in India can do so through "fly in, fly out" representation: they may fly in for temporary periods to provide legal advice but are not allowed to open offices in the country. In China, only locals can practice Chinese law, although international firms and

Chinese firms are finding ways to overcome this restriction. Brazil presents similar obstacles to foreign lawyers. Cross-jurisdictional legal work is strictly regulated. Foreign lawyers and international law firms may not practice law in Brazil except in matters of purely international or foreign law. While a significant and growing number of international law firms have established offices in Brazil, none of them are authorized to practice Brazilian law. Bar association regulations even prohibit foreign-qualified lawyers from working in the same firms that employ local lawyers.

The available information about law firms varies considerably globally. The US legal market enjoys a high level of transparency when it comes to law firms and is abundant with facts and figures. This transparency is in stark contrast to European firms that only recently started to report their number of equity partners but are a long way from reporting profits. It could be that in the United States, profit, as a measure of success, has a tremendous marketing value. Clients want a financially successful law firm because that must mean the firm is good. In Europe, it is still widely considered unwise to reveal to clients the level of a law firm's profit in case it encourages another bout of pressure on pricing. There is also no legal requirement for partnerships to disclose actual partner profits, a good enough reason for most European law firms to err on the side of caution and opt for discretion. *The Lawyer*, a UK magazine that annually provides an analysis of the top 100 European law firms, reports that it is not just the press that would find financial reporting by law firms useful; clients based in Europe are starting to call for financial information as well.[2] In a similar spirit of disclosure to the United States, some European-based clients have reported that they ask their firms for profitability data because a law firm should at least be able to run its own business successfully before it is entrusted with the business of the client. When I interviewed a number of general counsel from international corporates for a survey on commoditization in 2016, they all expressed annoyance at the lack of transparency in the pricing of law firms' services. Few law firms can break down their price proposals upon request, and none have a transparent profit margin. Increasingly, price transparency counts for a larger share of the point system clients implement in their panel appointment rounds. From the perspective of a general counsel, a long-term relationship is built on transparency. Many of them argue that companies in other sectors must disclose costs and markup in their long-term relationships with partners and suppliers, so why should law firms not have to do the same? The sentiment is that law firms should be subject to the same regime as their clients.

Having said that, the perception among several general counsel is that US law firms are more used to showing their numbers and that they are responding better to commoditization than are their European counterparts. Some general counsel provide examples of how US firms tend to allocate work more efficiently internally and perform the work in states where it is less costly, without compromising on the quality. Many US firms also have a greater ability to accurately quote and handle alternative fee arrangements.

THE US LEGAL MARKET

As headquarters for 134 of the *Fortune* Global 500 companies, the United States is the world's undisputed economic leader. This position, of course, is reflected in its legal market and the global dominance that the top-tier US law firms enjoy. The US legal market is rich in available data, to a large extent due to law firms' voluntary reporting. As pointed out in Chapter 2, "It's Not Like It Used to Be," the Legal Executive Institute estimated the size of the US legal market to be about $437 billion at the end of 2015, with law firms accounting for $276 billion of that number.[3] With a few exceptions, the leading law firms are concentrated predominantly in New York, with some in California, Texas, Chicago, and Washington, DC. When law firms in the upper-middle segment and upwards speak about the US legal market, they generally refer only to the "AmLaw 100"—the overview and analysis of the top-earning law firms in the US market provided by *The American Lawyer*.[4]

As in many jurisdictions, location determines the nature of the practice specialties developed by firms. Specialties are driven by the type of clients that are successful in that particular location. In the United States, Texas firms dominate the oil and gas industry. In Chicago, where manufacturing and railroads were historically strong, corporate advisory practices, including antitrust, and general litigation services are dominant. Washington, DC, firms reflect the proximity to government. New York–based law firms specialize in the finance-related work of their Wall Street clients. The technology boom of the late 1990s was serviced by California-based law firms taking the lead on advising the emerging start-ups. Even though strong US law firms wanting an international reach have shifted practice to New York, these origins of identity have never quite been abandoned.

Most US law firms' initial reasons for internationalization were to follow their US clients wherever they went, but only to practice US law. In the pre-Internet era, time zones mattered more and transnational communication was expensive. Communication involved a phone conversation that required both parties to be awake at the same time. For a US business executive sitting in Europe, having access to US law advice in the same day was quite valuable. With the further globalization of the economy and law, the top-tier US law firms used their reputation and quality to gain a global client base. An international identity of a US law firm nearly always includes a strong New York–based presence because New York epitomizes the importance of the United States to the international legal services market. The city serves as the financial center for the United States in the international market. Furthermore, to the extent that US law itself is significant in the international economy, it is nearly always New York law that matters. Members of the Global Elite are US firms, and all have a strong base in New York.

Government regulation of business activities is a pervasive feature of the US economy. In recent times, the Sarbanes-Oxley Act of 2002, following the Enron and WorldCom scandals, and the Dodd–Frank Wall Street Reform and Consumer Protection Act of 2010, following the financial crisis, have provided much work for US business law firms. The increased enforcement of financial regulations and of the 1977 Foreign Corrupt Practices Act (FCPA) has launched corporate investigation as a central practice area for most US business law firms. Threats from regulators is very high on the list of short- and medium-term concerns of general counsel today, according to the General Counsel Excellence Report 2015.[5] In 2016, the US Department of Justice, the criminal enforcer of the FCPA, saw a record-breaking year for FCPA enforcement with the highest number so far in terms of yearly FCPA settlement amounts. The number would be higher yet if the enforcement actions of the Securities and Exchange Commission (SEC) were added to that number. In particular, for banks, the enforcement actions of US authorities have increased. A recent study on the conduct costs of banks, carried out by the UK-based CCP Research Foundation and published in July 2016, tallies the total legal spend for the 20 biggest global banks since 2011 at £252 billion ($330 billion as per exchange rate in July 2016).[6] Although UK authorities and other authorities across the world help to enforce government regulations, the dominant enforcers are based in the United States. With regulators on the warpath, US law firms have had more work to meet companies' needs to stay on top of compliance.

EUROPE

Europe is the continent most populated by nondomestic law firms. Brussels alone is home to the representative office of close to 100 foreign law firms. London is also densely populated by representative offices of law firms from all over the world. Apart from the representative offices, foreign law firms have also established a real presence in many of the European jurisdictions, competing successfully with local firms. This process of internationalization in Europe was to a large extent initiated by the UK Magic Circle and Silver Circle (London firms closest under the Magic Circle firms), which quickly expanded to continental Europe upon the emergence of the European Union. As stated previously, the top 10 law firms dominating Europe's high-value transactional work are the Global Elite. The other firms that dominate European high-value work are the "national champions"—firms that are of such quality in their home country that they can attract high-value cross-border work. Seven markets in Europe generate 90 percent of the total European legal revenues: the United Kingdom, Germany, France, Spain, Italy, Benelux and, if taken as a whole, the Nordic countries. Let us take a look at each of these, as well as at China and Africa.

Europe is the continent most populated by nondomestic law firms

The United Kingdom

The United Kingdom accounts for around 10 percent of global law firms' fee revenue, making it by far the largest market in Europe, according to TheCityUK's UK Legal Services 2016 report.[7] Based on revenue, four of the top 10 AmLaw Global law firms are UK firms. The largest law firms in London also have more lawyers overseas (typically between 45 and 65 percent of their practitioners) than in their home base.

One-third of all people employed in the entire legal industry in the United Kingdom work in London. The UK law firms have a strong global position due to the English language and the popularity of English law. Some 27 percent of the world's 320 legal jurisdictions use English law. Around 40 percent of governing law in all global corporate arbitrations is English law. The position of the City (the financial district of London) in the financial world is of course another substantial factor. Between 2009 and 2014, the financial services industry accounted for 43 percent of the total value of deals among the top 50 UK City law firms. It remains to be seen to what extent Brexit will change the focus of the City law firms. Beyond the financial market, the United Kingdom is the headquarters of 26 of the *Fortune* Global 500 companies, placing it among the top on the list of countries.

City law firms are frequently subdivided into four broad categories: Magic Circle firms, Silver Circle firms, midtier firms, and American law firms with offices in London. Four of the Magic Circle firms, Allen & Overy, Clifford Chance, Freshfields Bruckhaus Deringer, and Linklaters, are among the Global Top 10 in terms of turnover. The fifth Magic Circle firm, Slaughter and May, may be placed at 51 on the Global 100 list in terms of turnover; however, in terms of profit per equity partner, it is among the top firms.

In the early 1990s, the Magic Circle firms emerged by reconsidering their relative focus in terms of practices and value. They had built a leading transactions business in the United Kingdom and then expanded this business into Europe and elsewhere, bringing about the initial segmentation of the market. They were riding on the back of the popularity of English law, the globalization of the City's financial services, and the trustworthiness of their dispute resolution institutions. In the past few years, the Magic Circle firms have been engulfed in a war for talent with US firms that have entered the City with an appetite for growth. There are 200 foreign law firms with offices in the United Kingdom, which makes it the world's most international market for legal services, and half of those are US firms. The US firms are entering the UK market with increasing aggression and speed. Davis Polk & Wardwell only took on its first UK-qualified lawyer as late as 2012. Davis Polk & Wardwell, Milbank Tweed Hadley & McCloy, and Gibson Dunn have recently underscored their commitment to organic growth in London by launching trainee schemes, some of which are among the highest-paid trainee schemes in the UK legal market. The full effect of this competition is yet to be seen, but the Magic Circle firms have all felt forced to overlook their lockstep system that prevents providing lucrative deals to lure rainmakers.

UK law firms also enjoy connections with Commonwealth jurisdictions. Over the past five to six years, a push has been made into Australia because the country often acts as a springboard into China and other Asian jurisdictions. It also has a wealth of natural resources that offer possibilities for growth. As mentioned in Chapter 2, London-based Ashurst merged a few years ago with Australian firm Blake Dawson and instantly gained a foothold in Hong Kong, Singapore, Tokyo, Shanghai, and Jakarta. Herbert Smith and Australia's Freehills voted to combine in 2012. The firm is now co-headquartered in Sydney and London. In recognition of the strategic importance of having an Australian capability in order to successfully develop an Asian practice, Hogan Lovells also opened an Australian practice in 2015. Likewise, Pinsent Masons opened its offices in 2015 in Melbourne and Sydney.

In the United Kingdom, the Legal Services Act 2007 came into effect in 2011, allowing nonlawyers in professional, management, or ownership roles to offer regulated legal services in England and Wales. The regulatory objectives of the Legal Services Act are, among others, to remove restrictions to competition. Several nonlaw firms have, under the Legal Services Act, been granted an alternative business structure license to provide legal services to clients. We may be seeing more players than just the traditional law firms emerging in the UK market in the near future. But the Legal Services Act also provides new opportunities for existing law firms. For example, the Act allows law firms to accept outside investment, which led Birmingham-based firm Gateley to become the first British law firm to float when it went public in 2015.

Having said all this, one significant cloud hangs over the UK legal market: Brexit. As the United Kingdom voted to leave the European Union in 2016, droves of UK solicitors rushed to register with the Law Society of Ireland. The Republic of Ireland is equivalent to the United Kingdom as a legal jurisdiction. It is English speaking, has similar legal institutions, and is a common law jurisdiction. Most important, Ireland is still part of the European Union, making it the destination of choice for solicitors in England and Wales, who are concerned about the consequences of the United Kingdom leaving the European Union. International law firms with their main European hub in London are reviewing their options, and some have already made moves toward, for example, Germany, in a bet that this is where some of the EU financial industry will move to. Others are not so worried. English law, the English language, and London as a hub for conflict resolution remain assets, whether inside or outside the European Union. Nobody knows what Brexit is going to look like and whether it will have any effect on the UK legal market at all. It might be a decade before we know.

Germany

The German legal market is dominated by firms with an international capability and their "friends." German firm Hengeler Mueller dominates the rankings together with Freshfields Bruckhaus Deringer (informally Freshfields), Latham & Watkins, and Linklaters. Germany has the second-highest number of international firms after the United Kingdom. Among them, Clifford Chance and Allen & Overy also have a strong position. A long list of international business law (IBL) firms, as well as German firms Gleiss Lutz and Noerr, service the midsegment of the market. In terms of fee-earner headcount, the five largest law firms are CMS Hasche Sigle, Freshfields Bruckhaus Deringer, Clifford Chance, Taylor Wessing, and Hogan Lovells.

Germany has 25 business law firms with more than 100 lawyers each; more than half of them have over 200 lawyers. Germany is the fourth-ranking economy in the world and, not surprisingly, home to one of the largest legal markets in the European Union measured by turnover. German banks and companies, both the very large ones and the famous Mittelstand sector, look beyond the borders of Germany. There are 28 *Fortune* Global 500 companies in Germany. Many of them, including Adidas, BMW, Deutsche Bank, Munich Re, Siemens, along with a number of other German global brands, are listed on the Frankfurt Stock Exchange and represent a turnover in the trillions. The IBL firms and the Magic Circle are successful in the German market. They come with an international capacity. Hengeler Mueller has responded to this situation by forming an alliance with London-based Slaughter and May, De Brauw Blackstone Westbroek (Netherlands), Bredin Prat (France), and Uría Menéndez (Spain). The increased size and internationalization of clients is often to the detriment of national law firms. The national legal work tends to shift in-house. *The Lawyer* reported in July 2014[8] that all in-house teams in the 30 major German companies trading on the Frankfurt Stock Exchange, which form the basis for the German stock index DAX30, had been increasing in size in the preceding five years. Commerzbank, Daimler, Deutsche Post, and Deutsche Telekom, for example, all employ over 200 lawyers in-house. BASF, Bayer, and BMW also do a significant portion of their legal work in-house. The high-level legal work they tend to procure is international, which means the firms with a global presence have an advantage.

There is another peculiarity of the German market. In most other European countries, law firms are concentrated in the capital. Nobody looks outside of London for a top-tier law firm in the United Kingdom or outside of Paris for such a firm in France. At the most, there will be a second important city in the same country in which top-tier law firms may have a presence, such as Barcelona in Spain or Milan in Italy. In Germany, this is different due to the individual strengths of the constituent states that make up the federal republic. Frankfurt, Munich, Berlin, and Düsseldorf, all located in different states, carry more or less the same weight. When Germany was formed in unification of the various German states in 1871, the newly formed country embarked on a major process of legal standardization. However, to this day, the various states have maintained their own laws to an extent that may contribute to the balance between German cities in the legal market and the lack of one epicenter. Frankfurt is the most important center for banking and finance in the German legal market, especially capital markets work, since it is home to one of the world's largest stock exchanges and many major financial institutions. After Frankfurt, Munich and Düsseldorf are the two most significant locations for the larger firms. Due to the enormous financial success of Bavaria, Munich is home to major banks and insurance companies, private equity and venture capital houses, as well as leasing companies. It is also a center for private trusts and intellectual property, with institutions such as the German and European Patents Offices and the Federal Patents Court. Düsseldorf historically grew to strength by being the industrial powerhouse of the Ruhr Valley and, as such, held particular strengths in high-end advice on corporate and stock corporation law. Düsseldorf is also home to an internationally well-respected patent court. The capital of federal Germany, Berlin, is lagging far behind other cities when it comes to legal importance. The capital is the home of many creatives, and the venture capital scene in information technology and software is becoming stronger. Apart from that, the proximity to government makes it a location for lobbying and advice on regulated industries.

Germany may not have any remaining connections with its colonial past that would bring the country opportunities in other parts of the world simply through language or cultural ties. However, many German law firms have good links with Eastern Europe, including offices in Eastern European capitals, due to their East German past.

France

France is the European Union's second-largest economy and serves as headquarters for 29 of the *Fortune* Global 500 companies, nearly all of them headquartered in Paris. This means that France has much room for competition in the legal market concentrated in one location. The French legal landscape is made up of a mix of domestic firms and leading international firms. The podium of French elite law firms exhibits Bredin Prat, Darrois Villey Maillot Brochier, and Gide. De Pardieu Brocas Maffei can also be counted among them. Gide remains the largest French international law firm, with some 600 lawyers worldwide. Law firm Fidal is the largest national French firm by headcount, with 1,200 lawyers spread over more than 80 offices throughout France. The leading international firms are Cleary Gottlieb Steen & Hamilton—which is widely regarded as the leading US firm in France—Allen & Overy, Clifford Chance, Linklaters, White & Case, and Weil Gotshal. France, and especially Paris, is a favored location for foreign firms seeking to gain a foothold in continental Europe. Among the business law firms in Paris, there are just under 40 international firms, mostly US and UK firms. Many of them have teams of fewer than 60 lawyers, who nevertheless occupy pole positions in certain areas of practice. Of the international firms, 13 have more than 100 lawyers. High-quality local boutiques are particularly prevalent in the French legal market, especially in contentious areas such as insurance, intellectual property, employment, and public law. But they also offer high-quality work in tax, insolvency, and midmarket mergers and acquisitions.

International firms had a strong foothold in France from early on, which meant that French top-tier law firms started off with a disadvantage when competing for international work

A little known fact is that Paris was the primary choice of location for foreign law firms wanting a foothold in Europe long before London became the hot spot. Coudert Brothers, a US law firm founded in New York in 1853, opened its Paris office, Coudert Frères, as early as 1879. It was in many ways the original international law firm: the first firm to open in many other countries around the world, including China in 1979. The firm dissolved in 2005 after a weak US client base and waning profits caused lawyers to abandon the firm's London and Moscow offices, rapidly followed by its New York partners leaving for Baker & McKenzie. White & Case, founded in 1901, opened its Paris office on Place Vendôme in 1926, long before its London office opened in 1971. Cleary Gottlieb opened its Paris office in 1949, just two years after the firm's birth in 1946. The city was its first choice for expansion in its initial steps toward becoming an international firm. International firms had a strong foothold in France from early on, which meant that French top-tier firms started off with a disadvantage when competing for international work. This might still be the case today.

French law firms also benefit from the historical tentacles of French colonialism. Currently, 21 African countries use French as their official language or one of their official languages. Seventeen of these countries have signed up for the OHADA Treaty, which provides for a uniform system of business law. The laws of these countries, sometimes referred to as *OHADA law*, are more in line with current French law, particularly corporate law, security interests, insolvency, and arbitration, areas that French law firms and the Paris offices of international law firms are well placed to profit from. Similarly, there is potential for French law firms in other former French colonies, such as French Indochina and parts of the West Indies.

Spain

Spain is the fourth-largest economy in the European Union, and eight *Fortune* Global 500 companies are headquartered in Spain. But Spanish law firms have access to a far greater market than the one within the borders of Spain. As much as US and UK firms have an advantage with regard to English-speaking clients, Spanish firms thrive in the rather sizable Spanish-speaking world. Numerous Spanish firms are establishing or developing a presence in Latin America, capitalizing on the increased focus on and investment in these regions. Another driver is the tendency of Spanish international companies to bring their preferred law firm with them wherever they go. A common history between markets provides not only a connection between language and legal systems but also longstanding business relations. The Spanish legal market therefore is dominated by four major domestic firms: Uría Menéndez, Cuatrecasas, Garrigues, and Gómez-Acebo & Pombo. Even though international law firms such as Clifford Chance, Linklaters, Allen & Overy, and Baker & McKenzie are all firmly established on the legal scene, Spain remains biased toward Spanish firms. The large Spanish firms also have another particularity: their founding partners, or their heirs, still work in these firms. This continuity has a strong influence on their culture, and they share many characteristics of family-owned businesses. The mindset of Spanish clients seems to have favored the international expansion of Spanish law firms.

At the Internation Bar Association (IBA) meeting in Tokyo, November 2014, I spoke to the general counsel of an international Spanish bank. He declared that the bank's Spanish law firm follows it wherever it goes. This is typical for these four major Spanish law firms and has enabled them not only to cement their place in the Spanish-speaking market but also to expand into the rest of the world either through offices of their own or through the use of best friends. Nevertheless, Spain continues to be an attractive market for international firms, as the recent arrivals of White & Case and Clyde & Co illustrate. In addition to full-service firms, Spain, like many other European countries at this moment, offers a number of highly specialized boutique firms operating in areas such as intellectual property, shipping, and wealth management. Many are well established, and others were recently set up by partners with years of experience at large, full-service firms.

There are 13 business law firms with more than 100 lawyers in Spain, and unlike in other European countries, some of these firms have a very large number of lawyers. Garrigues, for example, has more than 1,600 lawyers active in Spain, and Cuatrecasas has more than 800, followed by Uría with more than 400. However, more than in other European countries, perhaps more than in any country in the world, the legal arms of the Big Four accountants have a sizable share of the Spanish legal market. By headcount, they are large: PwC with close to 1,000 lawyers, KPMG with more than 600, and the other two not far behind. They might not be doing high-value work on capital markets transactions or mergers and acquisitions, and they are steering clear of nontax litigation, but in terms of revenue, they are closing in on the top-earning law firms.

Italy

The Italian market is dominated by strong national law firms, most notably Bonelli Erede Pappalardo, Chiomenti Studio Legale, Gianni Origoni Grippo Cappelli & Partners, NCTM, and Legance Avvocati Associati, the first three also being the highest-grossing firms in Italy. The full-service international firms are, however, also competing at the top, especially regarding finance work. Clifford Chance, Linklaters, Latham & Watkins, and Allen & Overy take turns in the top tiers of banking, finance, and capital markets. The successful business law firms tend to have a strong base in Milan and Rome.

Similar to Spanish firms, Italian law firms tend to still have their founding partners present and exhibit the culture of family-owned companies

Italy is one of the most over-lawyered countries in the world. According to the Council of Bars and Law Societies of Europe (CCBE), in April 2015, there were 246,786 lawyers registered with bar associations in Italy. Italy has more lawyers per capita than any other EU country. Even though there is such a high number of practicing lawyers, there are no large law firms comparable to what we find in France and Spain. There are around 113 business law firms in Italy, but only 11 of these have more than 100 lawyers. Only four of them have more than 200 lawyers. This might be partly due to the relatively modest size of the high-end corporate market and how clients prefer to engage their outside legal counsel. Similar to Spanish firms, Italian law firms tend to still have their founding partners present and exhibit the culture of family-owned companies. A large full-service firm may find it difficult to survive. Not many *Fortune* Global 500 companies are looking for a sizable law firm that can also follow them into the world. Italy further lacks the historical ties enjoyed by Spanish and French firms.

In August 2014, the new Italian Prime Minister Matteo Renzi announced a series of measures designed to overhaul the country's notoriously slow justice system. The BBC reported that a business that goes to court to enforce a contract can wait three years for a ruling—twice as long as in France. This kind of news perhaps feeds into the prejudices western countries tend to have about Italy. But Italy also has a very resilient economy and the third largest in the European Union. Italian products are still coveted around the world. While Italy's large industrial production may have suffered, it has a vast number of small and middle-sized goods manufacturers that can weather harsh economic times. Italy may have only nine *Fortune* Global 500 companies, but that is one more than Spain has. As elsewhere in Europe, top-tier firms in Italy mostly continued to grow since 2008. Many of the strongest performers relied on their domestic white-collar criminal practices, disputes, insolvency, and compliance advisory work.

Benelux

Looking at Belgium, the Netherlands, and Luxembourg, the Dutch market is perhaps the most dynamic one. Similar to the Spanish market, the top-level work in the Dutch market is dominated by national champions, with the exception of Allen & Overy: De Brauw, Nauta Dutilh, Stibbe, Loyens & Loeff, and Houthoff Buruma. Other strong performers are Freshfields and Clifford Chance. A fair number of IBL firms are also operating in the Netherlands, but they tend to handle the midtier work. The Netherlands is the smallest of the major EU economies, but it is the fourth-largest legal market in terms of combined law firm revenues. This market is to a large extent tax driven. Looking at the companies in the MSCI World index that are either domiciled in a tax haven or have at least one majority-owned subsidiary, one-fifth of those are headquartered in the Netherlands. The other most-used jurisdictions among the MSCI World Index are Cayman Islands, Hong Kong, Luxembourg, Switzerland, and Singapore. But whereas other European countries with attractive tax status, such as Ireland, Luxembourg, and Cyprus, do not have much of an economy of their own, the Netherlands does. It is in eighth place in the world in terms of exports and has a sizable trade surplus. Twelve *Fortune* Global 500 companies are headquartered in the Netherlands. However, a peculiarity of some of the industries that are traditionally strong in the Netherlands, such as agriculture, offshore and onshore contractors, and the oil and gas industry, is that these industries have traditionally always done much of their legal work in-house with very little external legal advice necessary.

By comparison, Belgium is a smaller market than the Netherlands but nevertheless a dynamic one. Where the Netherlands has 14 business law firms with more than 100 lawyers, Belgium has nine such firms, which is equal to Ireland and not far behind Italy. International firms as well as Benelux firms (Stibbe, NautaDutilh, and Loyens Loeff) have been settled in the market more or less since the late 1980s, and long-established national firms have to compete with internationally known brands in a number of practice areas. Business law firms Liedekerke, Eubelius, Van Bael & Bellis, Lydian, and Altius belong to the national champions. Looking at the top 10 list of law firms based on turnover, they are nearly all national or Benelux law firms, with the exception of Baker & McKenzie (third place) and CMS De Backer (ninth place). Benelux law firm Stibbe tops the list, followed by Belgian firm Liederkerke. Of course, Brussels is also a necessary address for many law firms that want to exude competence on the EU regulatory front; hence, many international firms have offices in Brussels.

The final member of the Benelux, Luxembourg, is an almost entirely tax-driven jurisdiction. Law firms focusing on tax will have an office in Luxembourg, since establishing a good relationship with the tax authorities there is key to helping the large international corporations who choose Luxembourg as their tax domicile. If one day the banking sector in Luxembourg were to fail, it would have no real economy to back the country up, much as Cyprus experienced in the 2012–13 Cypriot financial crisis. Nevertheless, Luxembourg has recently also proved popular with Chinese state-owned enterprises that tend to follow each other's lead and have chosen Luxembourg as their gateway to the European Union.

Scandinavia

Although we tend to speak of the Nordic market, when it comes to its law firms, it is really a case of individual national firms dominating their local markets. A number of consolidators have breached the surface and seem set to become pan-Nordic top players. Looking at the market value of publicly traded shares, Scandinavia as a whole would rank number seven in the world because the individual Scandinavian countries rank relatively high. There are four *Fortune* 500 companies in Scandinavia, of which three are located in Sweden. But the jury is still out on whether the pan-Nordic law firm would have a business case. Rochier and Hannes Snellman, for example, have respectively been making a push out of Finland, setting up shop in the other Nordic countries. Another example is Magnusson Law, a law firm that has quickly grown with nine offices in three years into a Baltic Sea Region player. The largest economic center in the region, Stockholm, is said to be difficult for international law firms to enter because it is necessary to have a comparatively large office to win business. The only Magic Circle firm to have an office in Stockholm is Linklaters, and it landed in the market in 2001 by merging with local firm Lagerlof & Leman. Other international law firms are

Baker & McKenzie and White & Case, but they are modest in size. UK law firm Ashurst shut its Scandinavian office in Stockholm in 2016. IBL firms may not be interested in having a large presence in the market. There are adequate numbers of quality national law firms to do referral work, and they have been hesitant to tie themselves up with best friends in order not to jeopardize this position. This means that there is an open and thriving market for referrals. During one of my visits to a Scandinavian capital, a partner with one of the leading law firms confirmed that they were reluctant to formalize a relationship with another law firm because they were, to a high degree, dependent on referrals.

CHINA

We tend to forget that a law firm is a relatively new concept in China. In 1993, DeHeng was one of the first People's Republic of China (PRC) law firms, founded by the state with the aim of professionalizing the legal market. Today, DeHeng is one of the leading PRC law firms, among many successful firms with high-quality practices. The same cycle that has been witnessed in the high-end manufacturing and electronics industry in China is also present in the legal sector. The Chinese lawyers who have been trained and employed by western law firms are returning to PRC firms. With ambition and know-how gained at some of the very best western law firms, they are helping the industry to professionalize at a rapid pace. PRC firms will increasingly move in on the territory of high-stakes international deals. Their service levels and ownership structures may not yet be up to the standards required by the large international corporates, but they soon will be.

China's legal market must be divided into PRC firms and non-PRC firms. Non-PRC firms are not allowed to practice Chinese law—restrictions prohibit all foreign lawyers from practicing Chinese law, including appearing in Chinese courts or in governmental hearings. You can broadly divide the type of Chinese client into two categories: state-owned enterprises and privately owned companies. They have different concerns, a different modus operandi, and totally different cultures. This also leads to strong regional law firms, as state-owned enterprises have grown strong in the separate provinces of China and tend to use strong local law firms. A decade ago, China was home to 19 *Fortune* 500 companies. This number had risen to 103 *Fortune* 500 companies by 2015.

The restrictions on the legal market make forging relationships with local Chinese law firms a necessity for international firms wanting to enter the Chinese legal market. In the beginning of 2015, Dentons announced plans to merge with mainland China's largest law firm, Dacheng, and instantly gained approximately 4,000 lawyers in the region. In 2012, law firm King & Wood, largely considered one of the top-tier firms in the country, combined with Australian firm Mallesons Stephen Jaques to form King & Wood Mallesons. In another manifestation of the convergence between the PRC firms and their international counterparts, Mayer Brown announced in July 2015 that it was to enter into an association with the Chinese capital markets firm Jingtian & Gongcheng via a joint international office in Hong Kong.

We tend to forget that a law firm is a relatively new concept in China

PRC firms typically have a different partnership structure from western law firms. Haiwen & Partners was the first top-tier PRC firm to adopt a western-style, pure lockstep system seven years ago and was until now the only one. It is more common for the partners in PRC firms to cooperate in name only and not to share a profit pool. This arrangement leads to difficulties with cooperation across borders. For example, a foreign firm that has to deal with the Chinese way of applying referral fees may struggle. These practices are legal in China but may not comply with the rules of a western bar association. Split profit pools also discourage cross-border referrals between partners. The Dentons–Dacheng combination (now Dentons) took the form of a Swiss verein, which may help to overcome the incompatibility of a PRC firm and law firms in other jurisdictions. Recently, Dentons's Chinese arm voted through reform that will see the firm move away from office-by-office profit sharing in China and establish five profit pools. PRC law firm Jun He (best friend with Slaughter and May) announced in 2015 that it had started a three-year trial run of a lockstep system for its profit distributions. At the same time, Haiwen & Partners decided to move away from the pure lockstep model to a more flexible version.

Foreign law firms with an inflexible lockstep structure have struggled to gain growth in China. A comprehensive overview[9] from the University of California–Berkeley on how international law firms are faring in China shows that an average of 12 international law firms opened a new office in China each year between 1992 and 2012. During that 20-year period, only 25 law firms withdrew from China because of a change of strategy. In the expectation that tomorrow's large clients will come out of China, many international law firms have taken a long-term view on their presence there. However, they seem to be overtaken by fast-learning PRC firms with a flexible reward structure that more easily rewards high-performing partners. In 2014, the average revenue growth rate among the 10 fastest-growing PRC firms reached 25 percent. Furthermore, according to deal data provided by Thomson Reuters, Chinese firms started in 2014 to outperform international rivals on the M&A league tables for deals involving a Chinese target company.[10] Also in 2014, the number of foreign firms in mainland China dipped for the first time since the country opened its door to nondomestic firms in the early 1990s, according to the official list published by China's Ministry of Justice.[11]

About three years ago, during one of my trips to China, I had a conversation with the general counsel of a privately owned Chinese car manufacturer. I was given a tour around the head office and its legal department with approximately 30 Chinese and non-Chinese lawyers. What surprised me in our conversation was that she revealed that in China lawyers have a low status compared to the status western law firms enjoy in western jurisdictions. In China, all legal expenses made by a company are seen as unwanted costs that should be kept to a minimum. Chinese companies still do not see legal advice as an investment. This explains what in the eyes of western law firms is sometimes baffling: why Chinese clients often pick the cheapest legal service provider with minimum regard for quality. Any law firm that has dealt with Chinese clients has experienced that they are very price sensitive, although that inclination has started to change. As Chinese companies grow increasingly international, with international investors or non-Chinese members of executive and supervisory boards to speed up the process, this view on legal advice will continue to change at a more rapid pace. Indeed, it is evident to everyone that China's legal market is in a period of rapid development.

The Shanghai Free Trade Zone (SFTZ) was launched in September 2013 as a free-market trial and testing ground for economic reform. The first joint legal operation in the SFTZ was announced between Baker & McKenzie and FenXun Partners in 2015. Since then, other international firms have been looking at the same possibility. In 2016, Hogan Lovells entered into a formal association with 170-lawyer Fujian Fidelity in the SFTZ. The zone is meant to offer access to foreign participation and investment in a range of sectors including telecoms, logistics, e-commerce, and finance, as well as law. The rules will permit Chinese and foreign law firms to set up joint operations in the area and mutually dispatch lawyers. Such a joint venture means that the non-PRC law firm can move beyond a mere representative office in China. I got indirectly involved in advising on some of the legal fundamentals underpinning the SFTZ. During the process, it became apparent that it was very difficult to get information on which objectives the zone was supposed to achieve. This vagueness in sources of rules and regulations is typical in China. Many Chinese have told me that it is intentional. I experienced the same when cooperating with a Chinese university on an anticorruption seminar in 2014. Being able to deduce clear rules for international companies operating in China proved very difficult. The rules are derived from a directive, which to westerners is very vaguely worded. Chinese lawyers and scholars are familiar with this vagueness and have a greater confidence in using it. In the western press, you see hesitant reporting unable to clarify exactly what the details are. Articles pretty much repeat the same vague statements made by Chinese government officials. Time will tell whether the possibilities of the SFTZ will work for foreign firms and gain favor. To quote Bill Gates, "We always overestimate the change that will occur in the next two years and underestimate the change that will occur in the next ten." It is likely to be a slow process, but it is safe to say that in 10 years, the market will be radically different. Much has already been achieved in the past decade by PRC law firms.

AFRICA

On the day that Bob Geldof released the fourth Band Aid single *Do They Know It's Christmas?* in charitable support of the countries hit by the Ebola outbreak in 2014, Ethiopia issued its first sovereign wealth bond. The two separate events, in my mind, represent the perception of Africa 20 years ago versus the reality of Africa today. Ethiopia is not the first African economy to issue a sovereign wealth bond. The Seychelles and Ghana became the first sub-Saharan country outside South Africa to issue bonds in 2006 and 2007, respectively. Since then, a string of other issuers has appeared, from Rwanda to Nigeria to Senegal. Africa today is a far cry from the continent it was only a decade ago. It has become the new economic frontier of the world not only in terms of natural resources but also in terms of infrastructure, consumer goods, telecommunications, and financial markets. Africa's risk–reward profile is developing at an increasingly rapid pace. Changing demographics brought about by, among other factors, a growing urbanized middle class, has made the rate of return on foreign investment in Africa today higher than ever before. Collaboration initiatives like COMESA, OHADA, and Africa50 have risen and are leading the way for other parts of the continent. China has taken a long-term view on Africa as a trading partner and is investing heavily in infrastructure projects in many parts of the continent. Future history books shall perhaps enlighten us as to how big of a part China played in Africa's development this past decade. I dare to wager that the progress of Africa seen in the past five or ten years will not be credited to the free water pumps or, often extortionate, microfinance initiatives launched by western economies.

On the day that Bob Geldof released the fourth Band Aid single, Ethiopia issued its first sovereign wealth bond

To approach Africa as if it were one legal market is to commit the same mistake that Band Aid has been criticized as making. The diverging experiences of African economies in the past decades have left the term *Africa* as a historical and oversimplified one. Attempting to summarize Africa's legal market in a short piece of text is impossible. Nevertheless, I will dare to point out distinctions based on my own experience. Looking at the legal market, it can be divided into North Africa, sub-Sahara Africa, and South Africa. There are countries that apply civil law and there are countries that use common law. In some countries, these systems operate alongside Sharia law and tribal or customary law. Another division can be made between Anglophone, Francophone, and Lusophone Africa. These areas tend to be influenced by foreign law firms from their respective mother tongue countries in Europe. French law firms have long been present in Francophone Africa but have in the past few years made a push in anticipation of its growing economy. The same can be said of UK firms in African Anglophone countries. Much legal advice by foreign law firms concerning Africa is being provided from the comforts of London offices, which is the center for the commodities trading market and where African companies tend to seek access to the capital market. However, law firms in many African economies are perfectly capable of handling their own business; others just need the time to mature. In comparison, China's legal market has moved faster, but China has a single government that is committed and focused.

The growing middle class in Africa is not evenly spread. The economic potency varies across the continent, as do natural resources and the level of democracy. Corruption remains an issue everywhere. The recent history of Africa's law firms is a story about natural resources, such as oil, minerals, and food. The Chinese realized in the past decade that in order to become a large taker of African goods, infrastructure was needed, and so they started to invest in and build railroads and roads on a grand scale. Improved infrastructure, among other factors, has led to an increased level of social welfare. It enables trade to thrive. As people get richer, their spending power increases. But although the physical infrastructure is improving, the financial infrastructure is still lacking. Since banks cannot offer the financial infrastructure needed, money transfer schemes, whereby people can use their mobile phones as bank accounts, have gained tremendous popularity. The most successful mobile-money system, M-PESA, is used by over 17 million Kenyans, and around 25 percent of the country's gross national product flows through it. M-PESA has been extended to offer loans and savings products and can also be used to disburse salaries.

Just as economies vary significantly across Africa, the quality of law firms also differs. Outside of South Africa, some of the most qualified law firms can be found in Nigeria, which also has the largest economy in Africa, with one of the most educated populations. During a recent visit to Lagos, Nigeria, I met with the five leading law firms as well as with some of the continent's largest banks. It quickly became apparent that the lawyers and bank managers are well educated, most of them in the United Kingdom. They are also smart, hardworking, and relatively young. Their internationally oriented outlook was also striking. London and Paris are two Nigerian hubs outside of Nigeria. All five law firms could tell me that they are stampeded by large western law firms that want to secure cooperation and become best friends. They constantly receive offers for free secondments as well as learning programs and so on. At the same time, they know that they will not take any offers that would eventually jeopardize the stream of referrals.

To be an actor on the world stage, you need lawyers with a number of years of experience. The smartest of students will not succeed without being trained in a good law firm. Local law firms in Africa simply have not had the time needed for training yet. Furthermore, the organization of their offices has been insufficiently honed to western standards. Foreign firms are apprehensive about settling due to corruption and the constant changes to rule of law. Some countries protect their market and forbid foreign law firms from practicing law. Although Lagos at the time of my visit, in my opinion, was relatively safe, even the local people thought I was very brave, or foolish, to visit because it was at the height of the attacks by Boko Haram. The expats of foreign law firms do not like that.

KEY POINTS

- The mosaic of different markets makes the legal landscape complex. Although business law firms across the globe might have more or less the same business model, the markets in which they operate differ significantly from each other. This disparity is important to understand in order to rule out the notion that a one-size-fits-all solution to law firms' strategies is viable. The strategy that works for one firm will not necessarily work for another firm. Legal business is not a case of copy and paste.

4

WHAT GOES UP

There is downward pressure on the price of legal services, and this compression will continue. In fact, it has only just begun. Two main factors have caused this squeeze: clients and commoditization. You may be thinking, "Hang on a minute, didn't I see reports on how legal fees are going up?" Yes, you probably did. This is related to either law firms and lawyers who do bet-the-farm work or lawyers who *think* they do bet-the-farm work but will soon find out that they do not. The truth is, rates are going down, except for the typical work of the elite law firms, where rates are going up. And not only are rates going down in the commoditized sector, the percentage of legal work that belongs to this segment is increasing. The bespoke segment is shrinking as the commoditized segment increases. It is already much larger than most lawyers realize. Most lawyers suffer from commoditization blindness. Many individual lawyers will make an error in judging their type of work. Hardly anyone does commodity work in their own view: it is all bespoke and complex. A 2016 survey on commoditization in the legal market, by TGO Consulting, asked lawyers from 100 business law firms across Europe if they recognized that the market was increasingly commoditized, and the respondents overwhelmingly said yes. At the same time, most respondents believed their firm was doing 70 to 80 percent bespoke work and only 20 to 30 percent commoditized work. Obviously, this does not compute. The reality is, bespoke work has a much narrower definition than most lawyers would acknowledge. While the effects of creeping commoditization have formed a grip on the legal market, clients' behavior has changed since beginning of the decade, especially after having been given a push by the 2008 crisis. They got smarter, better informed, and changed the way they work. Law firms are facing more determined and empowered general counsel, panel rounds, and the scrutiny of pricing directors, aided by e-billing and analytical tools and in competition with alternative service providers that have increasingly deep pockets. With these forces converging, price pressure on legal services is here to stay, and it will have consequences that most law firms are not yet aware of.

Most lawyers suffer from commoditization blindness

THE CLIENT CRUSADE

Long gone are the days when a company had a house lawyer—a single loyal and trusted law firm that fulfilled all its legal needs. Globalization and cost awareness have shifted the balance of how and where the legal work of a company is performed. Law firm panels have gone through a slimming process, and an increasing share of companies' legal work is done in-house. The in-house counsel of today has a different profile in comparison to 10 years ago. It is more likely to be a smart and ambitious professional, who often has past experience in a law firm. An increasing number of in-house lawyers know exactly how the pricing of a law firm works and what room there is for maneuvering. The global client not only has increased buying power because it can offer larger bundles of legal work across markets, but it also has increased negotiation power due to intimate knowledge of the pricing mechanisms of law firms.

Over the past five years, whenever you hear general counsel speaking, usually as part of a panel, they will relentlessly, at every appearance, hammer on one thing: prices must go down. And they mean it. When lawyers hear this, they nearly all think, "Yes, yes, but that doesn't apply to me. I have my clients and I do complex work." But as attributed to Ovid, *gutta cavat lapidem non vi sed saepe cadendo* (dripping water hollows out stone, not through force but by falling often). Persistence will eventually hollow out the stone.

Clients have spent the past five years backing up the vows made in public by general counsel. They have done so both on an individual level and by forming platforms in a concerted effort to become unified. The Corporate Legal Operations Consortium (CLOC) is one example. The ACC Value Challenge is another well-known example. It is an initiative by the Association of Corporate Counsel that provides training and resources for in-house counsel and their outside partners. General counsel at corporations such as Shell, Reckitt Benckiser, 3M, Pfizer, GlaxoSmithKline, and Bank of America form part of its steering committee. Members share best practices and tactics such as value-based fee arrangements, efficient use of technology, and process improvements. More important, they have a charter that members adhere to. This charter's single goal is to bring prices for legal services down. Law firms will describe this campaign differently, often emphasizing that the increased complexity of the law has led companies to improve working relationships with law firms and to help ensure that both parties clearly understand the value of working together. And yet, the ACC Value Challenge and similar initiatives simply come down to one purpose: pressing the price for what clients see as commodity work.

A long time ago, lawyers used to "weigh the file" in order to determine the price. More paper simply meant more hours and effort. As the regulation of business activities increased dramatically during the 20th century, legal work increased in complexity and became harder to price. Hourly billing allowed clients to understand the "product" that they were buying and compare it to other products in their own market. As the legal market grew, law firms needed measures to predict income, expenses, and budget in order to become successful players in that market. Billable hours can easily be measured, compared, and reduced to realization rates: comparing hours worked with the actual fees collected on those hours. They can also be used to guide lawyers' performance and evaluations. The time sheet that law firms brought in to keep a record of the "inventory" became the inventory itself.

Most firms break hours into pieces, typically charging clients for each six-minute accrual used by a fee earner. This method of adding up fees requires a degree of precision that is virtually unattainable. Nevertheless, lawyers and paralegals strive to record each telephone call, meeting, email, memo, draft agreement, research project, and document review. The result is relentless time-keeping, which occupies much of a lawyer's awake time. However, measuring legal services in units of time takes focus away from the value of the work produced and the results achieved. Few other industries would be successful if they measured productivity by the time their workers spent without regard for the actual output. Law firms are now standing on the fault line between the traditional pricing, based on the building blocks of time units, and the new approach of having to put a price on the value of their product. Already, the previously accepted habit of automatically adjusting the tariffs upward across the board at the beginning of each year is no longer tolerated. Likewise, the curious process of automatically increasing the rate of an associate at any point during a year simply because they have passed a certain date that means they are operating at a new level of experience will very soon be an antiquated method.

Alternative price arrangements have entered the market and are gaining favor with clients. In-house lawyers are used to the hourly rate and know how to work with this method to get close to what they want. They know that, at this point in time, stepping over to an alternative pricing method will lead to an insurance premium for the risk the law firm is taking. Nevertheless, alternative pricing methods are gaining ground both due to demand from clients and as a consequence of increased use of technology. As law firms are starting to use software to perform tasks, they will start to gain an understanding of pricing their services in ways other than by the hour. Alternative service providers are already masters of this approach to billing because they were never cast in the mold of the billable hour to start with.

For some reason, lawyers are prone to immediately agree to a discount when a client asks for one, much more so than in other markets

Royal Dutch Shell announced in May 2015 that it had appointed a partner from Reed Smith to analyze and manage its pricing arrangements with external law firms in order to rein in costs. It was a move to "put fee arrangements at the forefront of the way the company works with law firms worldwide."[1] Shell adopted a charter of alternative fee arrangements (AFAs) for all panel firms in June 2014 and, since then, no longer instructs any external counsel without an AFA in place. The hourly rates it pays today are part of legacy matters or hybrid fee arrangements. Shell announced that by implementing the AFA and hiring an expert to oversee the process, it hopes to bring its legal spend down by $9 million (still just a fraction of its total legal spend). More and more clients follow Shell's lead.

Alternative fee arrangements are not used merely to bring down costs; they are also attractive because they make cash flow and budgeting more predictable and are a tool for risk sharing. Many clients need a law firm to invest in a matter so that the ultimate cost will be related to the outcome. Consortia that bid for public–private partnerships projects, for example, want the cost of the legal part of the bid to stay limited in case the bid is not successful. The higher legal spend in case of success has been calculated into the bid, and the law firm gets a share of the benefits. The risk-sharing arrangements are also common in legal areas, such as mergers and acquisitions and litigation.

For some reason, lawyers are prone to immediately agree to a discount the moment a client asks for one, much more so than in other markets. Traders of goods or other type of services know their bottom line and where they must be pricewise. Their position depends on supply and demand, along with a few other factors, but the bottom line is the bottom line. For lawyers, this is a fleeting concept. The bottom line of each individual case is not calculated; it simply becomes a matter of making more hours. Once a discount is given, the price for the same services cannot go up again. The discounted rates become structural and are simply rates, albeit lower than planned. Discount sounds better than just calling it a "rate befitting commodity work." The habit of the individual partner agreeing to a discount also means that partners within the same firm risk charging different fees to the same client in a manner that is not correlated to the type of work. Differing rates may even be applied for the same type of work. The calculated confidence of a law firm's official rates will all of a sudden be exposed as mere confusion.

Alternative fee arrangements are agreements between a law firm and a client that determine the law firm's compensation, calculated using a structure other than hourly billing and based on the experience level of the fee earners. Alternative fee arrangements include contingency fees, fixed fees, value- or success-based fees, and other alternatives to hourly rates, such as hybrid fee arrangements. The discounted hourly rate, including volume discount and blended rates, is also often seen as alternative fee arrangements, at least by the law firms. The practice of pricing legal services according to their value—in relation to the client's exposure—is much more prevalent in the United States than elsewhere because the US market is still much more litigation driven in comparison to other parts of the world, where outcomes are monetary or can easily be monetized. The different outcomes in a litigation case, such as settlements or size of claims, are also relatively easy to identify and quantify.

In a contingency fee arrangement, the law firm receives its compensation as either a fixed or scaled percentage based on the outcome of a matter. These kind of "pure" contingency fees are more commonly used in the United States in cases where a plaintiff is seeking damages as well as in M&A transactions. In a partial contingency fee arrangement, the law firm receives part of its hourly rate plus either a smaller percentage of any recoveries in a lawsuit or a contingent on agreed-upon results or milestones being achieved. In a defense case, or when the result sought in the matter is not monetary, such as a corporate transaction, a holdback/success fee can be used. A portion of the law firm's fees are paid up front, and in the case of the successful completion of the transaction, the law firm receives a multiple of the holdback or an agreed-upon success fee.

Fixed fees are used when a law firm handles a matter or an ongoing specific type of work for a lump sum or for a certain fixed sum per month. Fixed fees are suitable only for services with a predetermined scope. Assuming the scope is possible to define, an equally sophisticated buyer and seller will end up with the right fixed fee. In such an ideal case, the client will not bear the cost of inefficiencies and the law firm can possibly earn extra by being efficient.

A law firm that does not have its bottom line minutely under control will suffer under a fixed fee agreement. Because law firms are not risk takers, nearly all of them build a buffer into such an arrangement. Most clients know this and see it as buying budget predictability. A retainer is usually a periodic (typically monthly) sum paid by the client in return for general legal advice as the need for it arises. This is especially used where the client requires ongoing general advice that is difficult to scope. The fees for legal services can also be capped. When a firm agrees to not charge for hours beyond a certain amount, the price has been capped. If work is completed in less time, the client will benefit by paying the lesser amount while not having to pay if the law firm's hours exceed the cap. Hybrid fee arrangements combine elements of various alternative fee arrangements.

Clients' in-house capabilities have improved, but it is important to remember that, in the eyes of the CFO, the legal department is still more or less just a cost. Under the label of legal spend, a company will bundle the cost of the legal department, the cost of outside legal advice, and any damages, fines, and so on. A large in-house department is a large cost. Like all costs, it needs to be justified and managed. In-house lawyers know that they have to warrant the space they occupy and the lack of flexibility in comparison to hiring external advisors on an as-needed basis. This means that a legal department has to maintain a delicate balance in relation to external law firms beyond the mere quality–price ratio. The price charged by the law firms must not be so low that it seems like a better alternative than running the legal department itself. At the same time, the in-house counsel have to show that they are getting the best rates and managing to cut invoices. Law firms and their lawyers still tend to think they are pivotal to the strategy of a company and serve as a partner in their most important operations. Typically, they are not. They are just cost—often a necessary cost, but nonetheless, just a slot in the profit and loss statement.

Granted, it is not always only a slicing of the rates that will please the client. Saving money for a client can take many different forms. Uncovering these parameters can be the key to a satisfied client. A lawyer needs to understand how the client perceives value. This perception differs for each client. In general, though, there is one thing that all clients consider the worst of sins: surprises. A head of legal of a listed *Fortune* Global 500 company whom I have known for many years has coined the term "PETT invoices," which is an acronym that expresses the core wish of every client. Legal services must be predictable, efficient, transparent, and timely. Of these factors, predictability is the most important. Being hit with a surprise in terms of legal spend is one of the worst things in the book of a general counsel. It is perhaps not so much a problem of the actual level of the legal cost as it is a matter of managing expectations. A law firm's estimate must be roughly on target, but even if it is not, a timely communicated overspend allows for some leeway. Communication is value for clients. Oddly enough, it is something most law firms will advertise they do well but somehow often fall short of in the execution.

Many clients have in the past years overhauled their legal panels. The requests for proposals (RFPs) they have used in the selection process leave very little room for law firms to express the quality or content of their legal advice. RFPs focus on cost and statistics that can be compared across the board. Often, the RFP is presented in an Excel spreadsheet. Apart from the rates and headcount, there is usually a series of questions, which invite standard value-enhancing answers and bland capability statements. "Describe how your firm intends to achieve the value goals of client." Er . . . by providing you with damn good legal advice at competitive rates? This really should be the answer preferred by a client because it potentially means receiving fewer lengthy, non-reader-friendly memos from such a law firm throughout its period of service. Instead, such questions are invitations to nothing but a spout of yodeling about "value propositions," being "client centric," and other guff. More neutrally worded, apart from the rates and discounts, these kinds of RFPs generate volumes of unhelpful data. Participating in such RFPs costs many hours and requires a considerable amount of resources. In the end, the rate card will be the only aspect the procurement department is interested in. In truth, the client already knows the legal quality it is looking for and where to can find it. Accordingly, many RFPs simply require a yes or a no answer to whether the law firm can provide services in certain areas, covering relevant jurisdictions, and the rest of the RFP is devoted to rates and alternative fee arrangements. An RFP is sometimes not even meant to be a chance for a new entrant but rather a tool to renegotiate the terms with preferred suppliers. It would in fact often be advisable for a law firm not to participate in the bidding process; however, the knee-jerk reaction to bid for work and quote a price is nearly impossible for lawyers to resist. But once you have discounted your price in a quote, you can never go up. Price is positioning, as I explain in Chapter 5, not a reward for work well done. The in-house lawyers handling your quote today will move on to work for your long-term client tomorrow, where he or she can inform the head of legal that the law firm the client has been loyally using for years quotes lower prices to new clients that do not even come with a guaranteed turnover.

Historic data in most law firms have been created merely to produce accurate invoices and tally the hours of fee earners

So, how have law firms responded to the changed clients? In the very beginning, prestigious law firms were true partnerships. The collective took precedence over the individual partners. Partners were "home bred," having climbed the ladder as a firm associate, steeped in its culture and traditions. The idea of pitching was distasteful. The way to attract clients was not by marketing or promoting oneself but by doing quality work. These were the days when big corporations did not pit one firm against another or shop around for lower fees.

Today, in response to the increased use of alternative fee arrangements, nearly every large law firm in the United States has hired a pricing director. It has become the full-time job of a team to work with spreadsheets using tools for profitability analysis. The team must mine past data generated by the law firm in order to understand the costs and appropriate packages of work. The pricing specialists will work closely with project management and business development to implement change. As much of a no-brainer as this may seem, it is far easier said than done. The historic data in most law firms have been created merely to produce accurate invoices and tally the hours of lawyers. All the parameters and coding needed to crunch the data and categorize the type of work within a file are either not there or have been entered incorrectly. Until an accurate data record becomes sizable enough to form the basis of value pricing, the pricing will have to be done on the basis of experience. A useful pricing director needs to have had

Mostly, when law firms speak about project management, it means they have sent some of their partners on a course

a long career in law firms and combine this experience with business acumen. All I will say is that some will be more talented than others and that resources will be scarce.

Another error that many law firms make is to focus on the partner rates, although this is rarely where the problem lies. Partner rates and firm profit are not directly linked. It will come down to the staffing on each particular matter. The problem for law firms is that although they may get into value pricing, their people are not value compensated. Associates are rewarded on the basis of the number of years' experience and a target number of hours. So they will produce hours, which is exactly what value pricing does not want. The law firm strategy may ask for one kind of behavior but promote another. A poignant example of what happens when you promote certain behavior has been provided by the corporate banks in the past decade: employees will do what they are paid for, not what they are told. Not that associates at a law firm will go on and fix the LIBOR rate. They will, however, produce in accordance with the given incentives and might end up hurting the firm as a whole.

With the increased use of technology and data, such as e-billing, corporate counsel can more easily track and assess outside counsel's performance—not merely its pricing but also its effectiveness and efficiency. With enough data created through an e-billing system, the creation of more accurate alternative fee structures will be possible. Fixed fees and success fees, or bonuses tied to performance, are meaningful once they are based on historical e-billing data to create benchmarks for average fees and results for specific types of projects. Clients' savings can also be monitored, something which is more difficult when using AFAs in comparison to the hourly rate. A majority of legal departments are now using e-billing software to these ends. At the same time, law firms are primarily using their accounting software for the management of alternative fees, which means they lag behind in information and lose the upper hand in price negotiations. Where the general counsel perceive that a service is suited to be estimated and handled under a fixed fee, law firms struggle with making this work. Legal media and lawyer conferences are busy discussing the potential use of artificial intelligence in legal services, while most law firms have not even solved their most basic software needs yet. Law firms' internal matters monitoring systems are entirely geared toward keeping track of time units. I know many clients that mistakenly receive an invoice for the hours spent even though a fixed fee has been agreed upon.

On the mechanical side of value pricing, law firms have responded by implementing legal project management. Alternative fee arrangements require management of schedule, risk, and cost in a rigorous and measured manner. But one must not be fooled by the smooth wording and obfuscating jargon that follows the description of legal project management in the media. In reality, except for certain parts of the US legal market, law firms have only just started coming to grips with legal project management. The largest firms began around 2011 to look into legal project management for one or more practice areas and some of those firms have since then proceeded to roll out project management for all practice areas. These are firms with resources and cases that warrant extra spend on overhead for returns on efficiency and risk management. For most other firms, when speaking about legal project management, it means they have sent some of their partners on a course.

Legal media and lawyer conferences are busy discussing the urgency of artificial intelligence, while most law firms have not even solved their most basic software needs yet

Value pricing means that if the client's perception is that the service is routine, then the price must be set accordingly. The key words here are *client's perception*, which is to say, not the opinion of the lawyer. For example, the legal advice given in most corporate transactions is routine; however, the lawyers work among many other consultants, most of whom charge a higher fee than the lawyer. In a corporate acquisition, the tone will be set by the investment banks, management consultants, and the Big Four. The corporate transaction lawyer can command a premium because of that. The same premium on price will apply to cross-border matters, especially where the City or Wall Street are involved. Billing rates vary significantly across the globe. In a joint bid involving several jurisdictions, the rates will diverge considerably, irrespective of the quality of the services. The firms outside of the economic centers in particular will take the chance of increasing their rates for such a cross-border bid. The brand value of the client may also lead to pumped-up rates. Law firms bidding to be on the panel of a *Fortune* Global 500 company will not quote a modest rate, assuming this client is used to higher numbers. Clients recognized this reputation billing early on, and in response, there are parties that offer anonymous tendering services for companies in need of legal services worldwide. They can confirm that the quotes they receive for the same work vary immensely, often without any apparent reason.

COMMODITIZATION: WHAT IS IN A NAME?

When a product becomes indistinguishable from other products of the same kind and consumers buy on price alone, it becomes a commodity. The quality of a given commodity may differ slightly, but it is essentially uniform across producers. In the financial markets, commodities are so interchangeable that they are traded on exchanges. In the legal markets, there will never be a trading platform, but the approach of clients in obtaining legal services has already changed. Commoditized legal work means it is work that has become so common that it will come at a lower price. Commoditization of law, in the form it takes today, entered the legal market as the rate of cross-border deals exploded around the year 2000. Before then, law was very local. Companies used a law firm in the jurisdiction in which they were headquartered, and switching law firms was seldom done. Law firms' interchangeability was close to none.

> *The problem is that a majority of business law firms still operate with business models created before the commoditization of law*

The unsettling part of this story is that the commoditization label fits the majority of all legal services today. Law firms just have not realized it yet. Nearly all general counsel I have spoken with acknowledge the increase of commoditization. They consider an increasingly larger chunk of their legal work to be commodity; many estimate that it is close to 90 percent. By this, they mean that the same type of work, which was not a commodity 10 years ago, is considered to be commodity work today. It would be a mistake, however, to think that commodity work is a bad thing that should be avoided. On the contrary, it can be highly profitable. However, it requires a different business model from one structured around bespoke services. The problem is that a majority of business law firms still operate with business models created before the commoditization of law. Lawyers have been indoctrinated to sneer at commodity work, not realizing the term describes something different today than when their opinion of it was formed. Commoditization is the perception that the client has of legal work. What is the level of interchangeability? Are there other lawyers or law firms that can do the same job? Commoditization has nothing to do with the quality of the legal services. An analogy with the medical profession would be that a general surgeon who performs an appendectomy is doing routine commodity medical work, whereas a neurosurgeon who performs a ventriculotomy is doing delicate, highly specialized work. But think about it—not just anyone can perform an appendectomy. A surgeon qualified to remove an appendix has many years of education and many more years of training and experience. The general surgeon is doing commodity medical work because he or she can easily be replaced from the large pool of providers who can attain equal results. The number of neurosurgeons is far lower, which puts their services on the more bespoke end of the spectrum. Likewise, commercial airline pilots have long recognized that their services have become a commodity. They may have a difficult job with much responsibility on their shoulders, but they have become easily replaceable and have seen salaries deflate accordingly.

Just because a matter is not a bet-the-farm type of case does not mean it is necessarily pure commodity work. There is a gradient between pure commodity work and bet-the-farm matters. This is where innovation distinguishes practitioners and their firms. Coming up with new solutions to problems that will not necessarily save a company from its downfall but that will help to change an industry is highly bespoke work. For example, Allen & Overy created a new holding instrument under time pressure during the Greek banking crisis in 2015, which allowed Pireaus Bank to recapitalize instead of going into a managed failure process with the risk of contagion across the Greek economy. In order to save the bank, bondholders had to be persuaded to swap their debt for equity, but because some bonds were held by public investors, an approved prospectus had to be attached to any new offer. By inventing a new holding instrument, a form of nontransferrable receipt, the legal obstacle of having to produce a time-delaying prospectus at launch could be circumvented and everyone could concentrate on the exchange offers instead. As far as legal work goes, creating and implementing this solution was well removed from being a commodity. However, this type of work is not done every day. Fewer lawyers than expected are difficult to replace. One of the hardest struggles will be for lawyers to get their head around the concept of commoditization and realize what type of work they really do in order to adopt a successful business model. Commoditization is no longer a dirty word.

Commoditization also does not refer to the accessibility of legal services. The entrance of computers and automation into the field of law has made many simple legal services accessible to everyone. Legal services consumers who use one-size-fits-all online forms to generate products such as wills, trusts, leases, incorporations, and template contracts are essentially basing their "shopping" decision on price only. In my view, this kind of commoditization will gain further ground, but it will not take over the legal profession. As expressed previously, a lawyer cannot be replaced by computers no matter how commoditized his or her services are. My use of the term *commoditization* refers to legal services and their level of uniqueness or the lack thereof.

> Commoditization *is no longer a dirty word*

Companies maintain two lists: law firms associated with routine matters and those used for occasional bet-the-farm matters. The first category is placed on the company's legal panel. When a bet-the-farm matter comes along, all panel agreements fly out of the window and no longer apply. In such cases, only a few law firms come into consideration, and the price is hardly ever an issue. Everyone else will more or less fall into the category of commoditized work, no matter how many tiers of increasingly complex work the legal panel's expertise is divided into. Commoditization has been one of the largest influences on price in the past few years. If a matter does not contain a large chunk of bespoke elements that require a specific partner, but instead can be placed with a number of alternative partners, it is commodity work. Today, the law firms of the entire middle segment of the legal market could be substituted for any of their peers. They are supermarkets, and it does not really matter which supermarket a client goes to. Perhaps the one has a more convenient location, while the next is a little bit better in vegetables; other than that, they are interchangeable. Clients' groceries can be purchased in any of them. The price pressure in this segment is enormous because there are many players. A decade ago, any lawyer doing securitization was a specialist. Today, securitization is routine work. Any M&A transaction below $250 million is commodity work, and many above this price level are also considered commodity. In a similar fashion, many other categories of legal work have moved into the segment of commodity, and most lawyers will have moved with them—only they will not have realized this. Individual partners will not recognize their own work as commodity work. First of all, simply being a partner means that you are a specialist. Each matter is bespoke and takes a level of ingenuity and innovation. Surely, this is not commodity work? Insurance claim handling is commodity work, or employment contracts perhaps: processes that can be outsourced or qualified in accordance with a template and processed by less-skilled lawyers or even nonlawyers, *that* is commodity work! I am afraid that a much larger part of all legal services than most lawyers can imagine is in fact already commodity work. Again, this is not to be looked down upon—it simply requires a different business model.

KEY POINTS

- Large parts of legal work have become commoditized over the past decade. *Commodity* means that, from a client's perspective, many lawyers and multiple firms can perform the same task equally well. This trend will continue; ever-more legal work will become commodity from the client's perspective

- Clients have become more cost-conscious. Commoditization and increased competition in the legal market give them the upper hand. Downward pressure on the price of the vast majority of legal work will continue.

5

POSITIONING

The position of a law firm is the sum of the characteristics that the market ascribes to that firm. Position is determined through the eyes of the client, and to a certain extent by peers, not by the law firm itself. It is formed by many different aspects—a mosaic of smaller and larger pieces. This chapter attempts to describe the most decisive aspects of a firm's identity as well as do away with the most persistent decoys.

The market of business law firms can be seen as a pyramid divided into three segments. At the bottom section of the pyramid is the large volume of low-end bulk commodity work. The midsection of the pyramid comprises law firms doing commodity work ranging from fairly complex to relatively standard bread-and-butter work. The tip of the pyramid is the domain of law firms handling the bet-the-farm work. The harsh truth about this pyramid is that the dividing barriers between the segments are one-way valves: a firm can slip down to the layer below, but it is nearly impossible to break through to the layer above. If a firm is seen by the market as one that handles lower-end commodity work, then this firm will seldom be given work from a higher segment. One of the most obvious ways in which we can see where clients position law firms is in the formation of their panels. As explained in Chapter 4, "What Goes Up," companies

It is pointless for a firm to pitch outside of its segment

will fill their legal panels with law firms from the bottom two segments of the pyramid. These firms will handle the more or less routine matters. Clients keep a separate list for bet-the-farm work.

The general counsel of a *Fortune* Global 500 consumer electronics group explained the group's panel firms to me. He willingly announced that the company is the happiest with the law firm it employs for all its housekeeping work. He explained how the legal departments at his company's headquarters and this law firm exchange lawyers regularly and work in an almost fully integrated way. Some lawyers from the law firm even hold office in the company's legal department for two days every week. They organize educational programs and events together, and the company is extremely pleased with all aspects of the law firm's services. It is a true partnership based on deep trust. And yet, whenever a more complicated matter containing strategic elements comes along, this matter goes to another law firm from the league of national champions. When a matter with an international dimension occasionally emerges that is important to the board, the company contacts one of the Global Elite firms to do the job. No two ways about it: the ceiling is screwed shut. This division of work cannot be overthrown because clients will not gamble. They will never be the first to trust a law firm with sensitive work such as crucial financing, a big M&A project, or a corporate investigation. If anything goes wrong, no client will want to explain to its shareholders why an untested law firm was chosen for this type of work. This also implies something that law firms have a hard time acknowledging: you cannot pitch for this type of work. It is pointless for a firm to pitch for work outside of its segment.

Law firms have a tendency to be blind to the type of work they actually do. Most law firms are "leading in mergers and acquisitions," for example, while there is absolutely no outward sign that this is true. The work a law firm does in reality will correspond to its position. Facing the truth about what work is actually performed by the firm's lawyers is a first step in understanding how a position can be influenced. This is why a law firm must be very candid in its self-assessment. For a start, taking a look at the number and size of files closed in the past 12- or 24-month period will say a lot. A high volume of small files and no file above $100,000 will tell a law firm that its lawyers are most probably doing bread-and-butter commodity work. If a firm in reality is performing small M&A deals while waiting for the big ones, that firm is not leading in M&A. Furthermore, the size of the various practice groups will tell the truth. If a law firm, again, claims it is leading in mergers and acquisitions, then this should be one of its largest practice groups. Mergers and acquisitions is an example of a practice that needs a large number of people in order to put together a team fast and handle multiple cases at any time.

So many firms are supposedly leading in mergers and acquisitions because this practice area tends to be treated as the Holy Grail: it is seen as a practice area with special powers that bring glory to its firm. It is the practice area with the most visibility. Numerous media and databases, such as Mergermarket, Bloomberg, and Thomson Reuters, keep track of and publish league tables on mergers and acquisitions. An M&A deal will often make the headlines in the morning press. It is the only practice area that takes its lawyers out of the office, not counting the ones that have to go to court, as they will be part of a team that includes investment bankers and management consultants. Even though it is a practice area that, for the most part, does not require great legal skills, it is often staged as part of a glamorous world. But each deal is like a firework exploding in the night sky. Once it has awed its audience, full of sound and fury, it extinguishes, vanishing from the night sky and people's minds.

Positioning is often confused with minimum requirements that law firms must have for their particular segment. Lawyers tend to put forward "excellent knowledge of the law" as a differentiating factor. It is not. Every law firm within the same segment has the same knowledge of the law. Boasting of business-oriented solutions falls into the same category of minimum necessities. There are myriad other examples of qualities that are mistaken for indicators of positioning. All such attributes are entry tickets to your segment but will not be the badge that proves your position. It is simply the code of the category—the minimum requirements of the segment to which you belong. A luxury car cannot boast of leather seats or electronic climate control because these are minimum qualifications for being a luxury car. Minimum qualifications are constantly mistaken for factors that determine position. Few questions make a law firm more nervous than "What differentiates your firm from your competitors?" It will cause partners to frantically search for what this really means and how their firm is different. It is a nonsense question and usually produces answers involving value–price ratio and expertise—all the things that are merely a ticket to the game. The best answer would be: "Not much differentiates us from our peers, and that is a good thing. Now, let's talk about how we would solve the legal matter at hand."

For law firms not positioned at the top of the pyramid, clients are more tied to the name of the law firm than to any of the individual partners. This is due to the nature of commoditized work. It does not matter too much which partner performs the work, and he or she can easily be replaced with any other partner from that firm. The higher up in the pyramid a law firm is, the more tied to a specific person the work is. The client will be reluctant to substitute one partner for another. This translates back into what a law firm can best spend its positioning efforts on. To whom is the particular client loyal—the firm or the individual partner? A law firm busy with low-end commodity work can better build on its brand name than waste efforts promoting individual partners. The higher up a law firm finds itself in the pyramid, the more it will need to pay attention to each partner's reputation.

The price a law firm applies to its services is a powerful positioning tool. It is a known fact that humans tend to use price as an indicator of how valuable a product or service is going to be. We have a psychological bias that depreciates a product if it is inexpensive or less expensive than other similar products. Price plays a role in the decision process of a buyer. Consider going to a large appliance retailer and standing in front of the wall of washing machines. Chances are, you are not an expert on washing machines and so you have to use price as an indicator. You use price to help you judge quality. It seems likely that a cheap washing machine is also a low-quality washing machine. It may have fewer settings and be made of cheaper materials. An expensive washing machine is generally assumed to be of high quality with lots of features and solid construction. The same goes for nearly every product and service. Even the price of bottled water will trigger the same reflex. Nobody is excluded from the positioning effect of price.

As the manager of an investment fund once told me, he had a much easier time getting investors when he arrived in his chauffeur-driven Mercedes than when he arrived in his wife's Peugeot.

A law firm lowering its rate—even under the guise of discount—will have positioned itself in a lower segment

In a similar manner, the prices that a law firm charges will influence the perception of the quality of its services. The hourly rate will communicate the quality of a lawyer's services and for what type of matters a client should hire this lawyer. The hourly rate is the scale by which lawyers measure their position. The price of a law firm's services will correspond to the segment in which it finds itself in the positioning pyramid. Contrary to what many lawyers might believe, the price is not just the consequence of the segment a law firm is in, it is also one of the very factors that have placed it there. This is why it is deadly for a law firm to structurally quote a lower price when bidding for work just to get a foot in the door with a new client. A law firm lowering its rate—even under the guise of discount—will have positioned itself in a lower segment. Panel round by panel round, pitch by pitch, it is a slippery downward slope. Lawyers have a tendency to immediately agree to a discount the minute it is mentioned by a client. Shooting yourself in the foot is all the more painful remembering you will not be able to go back through the door you have shut. It can easily be likened to the business of commercial real estate. For commercial real estate, the most important factor is to keep the rental price per square foot on course. In bad times, they tend to first offer rent-free periods or give away goodies rather than lower the square foot price. The same applies to lawyers: it is better to do work for nothing or give away goodies than to lower the hourly rate. Law firms might say, "It is either lower the rates or see all the work go to competitors!" Indeed, the price of a law firm's services filters the work it will be awarded. Partners with an above average hourly rate will not receive routine work. Commodity work will, by its nature, not be worth it. If a law firm has the strategy of positioning itself in the high-end commodity segment, then it had better stand its ground in a shoot-out. When eventually the smoke clears, such a law firm will still be standing, enjoying the view over its competitors in the segment below.

Of course, a law firm can lower its rates with the aim of tackling a new segment. Lower price segments with more commoditized work can be highly profitable. In such a case, the image of the law firm must follow. An office address in the most expensive business district, and all that comes with it, is contradictory and confusing when used by a law firm in the segment that comes with lower prices. The positioning effect of price does not mean that law firms should artificially increase their rates in anticipation of having to give discounts. It is misguided to start off with such a lie in any client relationship. A law firm is out to build a relationship of trust with the client.

Taking a look at the personal address list of a partner in one of the law firms in the top segment of the pyramid will probably tell you that he or she is dancing cheek to cheek with the captains of industry. The network of a law firm's partners positions the firm. The partners of a top national champion are usually the prime example of this. Contrary to common beliefs held among lawyers, it is not a question of being in the right tennis club or playing golf. No matter how well you play or how charming you are, it will not get you bet-the-farm work. Networking at this level has to be linked to the right context; it needs to directly build on a business reputation. Shaking hands and making small talk at receptions will not help you. In fact, too many receptions are damaging. This type of networking needs to be connected to your standing within your profession and the message you are trying to convey.

Name dropping does not help positioning. Every law firm in the middle to upper segments of the pyramid has at some point worked for the big names such as McDonalds and Deutsche Bank. As we know, these companies will have all level of law firms providing legal services ranging from highly commoditized to unique. It is the type of work that counts along with the length of time that a firm has serviced that client. However, analyzing the client base of a firm will speak volumes about a firm's position. What is the profile of the total client portfolio? Which type of industry or type of company is dominating? If a firm is a leader in mergers and acquisitions and an analysis of its client portfolio shows a majority of representatives from the insurance industry or real estate sector, then reality displays a different picture from what the firm proclaims. Likewise, if a firm is a leader in energy and only 10 percent of its client portfolio is from this sector, then clearly it is not leading in energy. Positioning is a conscious and continuous process. Individual partners can easily and unknowingly position themselves in a segment they subsequently cannot get out of. Lawyers are scared of an empty desk and will be driven by this worry to take most cases coming their way. If a lawyer keeps taking cases indiscriminately, he or she will build an unwanted profile that does not fit the firm. Case allocation is a tool to control this poor practice, but it is a sensitive topic. The partner that a client happens to contact will usually handle the case. But often a case may be better suited for someone else's profile. A case allocation policy ensures that profiles are driven at a firm level. A strategic M&A lawyer can better pass on a private equity deal to a colleague partner whose profile is tuned toward private equity. Even though the lawyer's M&A profile may not stand to lose due to handling the odd private equity deal, the profile of his or her private equity colleague will gain proportionately much more. Consciously building a profile is important because it provides the best chance for a lawyer to stick out above the rest in his or her field. If various matters are spread willy-nilly among partners, then no one will be able to build a strong profile. This will negatively affect rankings and positioning. Strong individual profiles are better for the firm as a whole.

> *Individual partners can unknowingly position themselves in a segment they subsequently cannot get out of*

I referred earlier to decoys in positioning—tools that masquerade as a means of influencing positioning. There is a whole media industry that feeds off the insecurity and lack of understanding of marketing that is prevalent among lawyers. An entire biotope of legal publications, thriving in and around a reef of law firms, has grown on the incapability of lawyers to evaluate media. Most gratuitous publications are nothing but vessels of paid-for-play articles and have little or no editorial content. More important, they have no readers. Some are veritable scams. Each sizable law firm is on average contacted twice a week with the offer of a tombstone, having an article written for a fee or simply paying for an advert. The entire law firm is actively approached by more than a hundred different publications per year. Many of them belong to the same publisher but operate under different names, presumably to cast a bigger net. Their method always plays on human vanity. The partner in question has been crowned a winner in his or her particular field of expertise by means of a client or peer voting system or by dubious or nonexistent research. To commemorate this victory, the partner is offered a chance to participate in various ways in the forthcoming issue of the publication—all with a price tag, of course. Sometimes a big name—typically a top-tier US or UK law firm—is "in the lead" of a content-driven publication and used as bait. These sorts of publications may have serious content but still no readers. Lawyers, however, love it, and they spend time and money participating without giving a serious thought as to which client out there would be eagerly anticipating such a publication. Not only that, most lawyers don't stop to think whether they have ever seen a law firm worth its salt advertise or participate in pay-for-play articles. The excessive media campaigns by Brobeck and Howrey back in the day were made using serious publications with an audience, and still the ads were foolish and did not work. The peddlers of these publications know to target partners directly because it is important to avoid a marketing department or anyone with more knowledge or an overview of the budget. Any English-speaking, eloquent salesman will have painted such a rosy picture of exposure and reputation that enough lawyers are ready to jump in with both feet, time and time again. It is nearly impossible to stop this circus of nonsense. This is not to say that participating in serious publications is not important. As explained previously, partners in the high-end commodity segment and above would do well to publish academically or to write opinion pieces in a reputable business newspaper. Building on a personal reputation becomes more important the higher up in the pyramid one is, since at this level lawyers become less interchangeable. The less commoditized work awarded by clients is more bound to the individual.

Although the legal market is awash with dubious platforms for the display of idle lawyers, there are a few serious players out there with a relevant purpose. Certain so-called client guides that provide yearly rankings of practices and individual lawyers have managed to maintain in-depth quality research and a commitment to reporting integrity. Chambers and Partners, IFLR1000, and Legal500 are a few examples. They often have a comprehensive view of the marketplace in each jurisdiction. There is no cost involved in law firms providing these guides with submissions and getting ranked. The business case of these publications rests on paid-for firm profiles that firms voluntarily want to place in the guide books and on ancillary services and events.

Law firms are invited to submit a summary of the most significant facts about each practice during the past 12-month period. This involves quite a bit of time and effort on the part of participating law firms. There is a prescribed format for each submission, but the tricky bit is to translate the unique or noteworthy aspect in each legal matter into a short description. This task is easier said than done. First, it takes both knowledge and oversight of the particular market in order to place each case in context—*why* this is new and unique. Second, formulating it clearly is something lawyers have a problem with. Lawyers write legal memos that chronologically build toward a conclusion. They have a tendency to find all legal details important along the way while overlooking important circumstances that are necessary. More important, they tend to be unable to summarize and highlight *des Pudels Kern*—the essence of a matter. The description has to hone in on the very core of the problem solved—*what* is so special. Third, the submission has to convey the predicament of the client. Lawyers tend to focus on the legal problem that was handed to them instead of presenting it from the client's point of view. There needs to be a business case and an identified opportunity cost. Something was at stake. Defining what disaster was averted through legal tools will immediately give evidence of the level of trust the client has placed in the firm, positioning the deal as far up the pyramid as possible. Finally, lawyers tend to focus on the written submission and pay too little attention to the clients they can submit to give reference to their work. The most decisive and impactful way of ranking a lawyer or practice group is through interviews with clients and peers. By picking out and preparing the satisfied clients that are willing to endorse the work done, a law firm can increase the impact of its submission.

The client guides rank lawyers and law firms on several factors and considerations, such as legal knowledge and experience, all of which are investigated by full-time employed researchers. The researcher for a particular jurisdiction will contact lawyers and clients directly by telephone and email. A law firm ranking in each particular practice area relates to a department of the firm, but individual lawyers may also be ranked in each practice area. When the research is done, the internal meetings are held by researchers, deputy editors, and editors to go through the research and compile and approve the ranking tables.

I am taking time to explain the workings of these client guides because they fill a not unimportant role in the positioning of a firm. Lawyers tend to think these client guides are for clients. But this is the same naivety that underlies their belief that clients will read any other publications about law firms. They will not. At best, clients will find it reassuring to hear about a first-tier ranking, referred to by the law firm itself in a pitch. Their real value comes down to the fact that client guides are revered by lawyers because they agree among themselves that they are a pretty accurate measure of where peers stand in relation to each other. They function as external and objective tallies alongside the hourly rates and the profit per equity partner, which will be used in cross-border referrals and the lateral hiring of partners. For lateral hires, the rankings based on firm size and numbers, such as AmLaw 100 and European Top 100, are also used. A client guide is a first, and sometimes the only, source that is consulted when confronted with an unknown party in a multijurisdictional deal. It is used as a reference when convincing a client of the choice of a local law firm in a jurisdiction the firm has no experience with.

The function of client guides goes further than being a weighted sounding line for each pool of law firms. If you mark out the rankings of a particular law firm in a spider diagram, where a tier-one ranking would be at the outer edge of the web and a nonranking would be at its center, you will get the particular fingerprint of that firm. This can be compared to the fingerprint of other firms. I wrote previously in this chapter how law firms tend to be blind to the work they really do—calling themselves a leader in mergers and acquisitions while the largest team in the law firm can probably be found in another, less glamorous practice. The ranking fingerprint will provide a fairly accurate picture of a law firm's real work and who the firm really is.

The difference between a firm that is ranked second-tier in M&A and capital markets and first-tier in dispute resolution and intellectual property and a firm that has the opposite ranking, may seem arbitrary. Nevertheless, they are two totally different firms.

Legal awards fall into the same category as publications: some of them are worth something, most of them are nonsense. Just as there are valuable publications in the market, there are also serious awards based on the findings of a proper jury. The American Lawyer Awards, The Lawyer Awards, the Chambers Awards, and the FT Innovative Lawyer Awards can be counted among them. These awards are handed out by informed observers of the market and based on extensive research, aided by an objective and discerning jury. Of course, the shortlists are long because they have to sell tables at the awards ceremony, but this does not detract from the value of the award itself. It will, similar to a high ranking in a client guide, influence the perception firms have of each other and sometimes even the perceptions of a client. As pointed out previously, position is the perception of a law firm determined through the eyes of clients and peers.

Lawyers will also be approached to speak at various events and conferences. Contrary to participating in a reputable publication, being a speaker or panel member at a conference almost never adds to the reputation of that individual. It might at most add to the brand recognition of the law firm. Even the position of being a keynote speaker is usually pointless. Unless a speaker has something memorable to say and is an above-average talented speaker, it is better that he or she does not participate.

> *In applying law, we use the concept of* bonus pater familias. *In practicing law, we can better use the standard of the trusted boardroom advisor*

Finally, as a last point in this chapter, here is why a law firm's lawyers should not be driving a Maserati or a Lamborghini, even though they could afford it: because all the small details add up to the positioning of a firm. Many small aspects will reflect and confirm a law firm's position and can help to build it. If a detail is overlooked, it can be damaging. In applying law, we use the concept of *bonus pater familias*. In practicing law, we can better use the standard of the trusted boardroom advisor. Driving a supercar is not what the discrete, trusted boardroom advisor does. If a lawyer has a career in criminal defense, then it might be a different matter, and a Ferrari will be just fine. So too can other practice areas provide some leniency in the choice of attributes, such as the practice of real estate, perhaps. However, on the whole, large, expensive watches fall outside the category of the trusted boardroom advisor. Discrete expensive watches are more in line with it.

Of course, positioning is more than just dress code. It is a summary of what a firm does and where it is visible. For example, a look at the total list of the topics of the seminars a firm has organized will be telling. A law firm intent on profiling itself in corporate transactions and finance must ensure that these are the topics around which their lawyers are visible. It is counterproductive if, at the end of the year, a yearly review reveals that most of a firm's seminars and events have been in energy or environmental law or any other non-core practice area, simply because fee earners active in those areas happen to be more industrious.

The same applies to the matters you choose to highlight on your intranet and website. A total overview must show a qualified majority of successful cases and articles in the firm's core areas. If you are a firm that wants a high profile in patent litigation and your employment law group is the most avid publisher on your intranet and website, then the PR campaign your firm is conducting in reality is contradicting your strategy. I include the intranet and not only a firm's website in this reproach because the focus of a firm's message must be not only external but also internal. Associates and other fee earners must be given the same picture as anyone else. It is a picture they will carry with them as they depart to another law firm and eventually will use when rating the firm as a peer in client guide research.

In the same way, positioning is not only how a firm's clients are met in the reception or what refreshments they are given in the meeting room; it is also how the office looks throughout and the type of food that can be found in its lunch room. Positioning is also how legal pieces are written, not just the quality of them. Are they academically structured and worded, or are they practical and to the point? Whichever the choice, it must be consistent across the board and in line with the firm's positioning strategy. A law firm's website is very often something its lawyers focus on. It is the most direct and available way of seeing what the firm is broadcasting to clients. And yet, for all the attention it gets from partners in the firm, it very often misses the mark. A website is no different from the other elements that reflect a firm's position. It has to confirm the law firm's position in a clear and confident way. It has to adhere to the standard of the trusted boardroom advisor. It is *not* a vessel of as much information as possible on what a law firm can do.

As pointed out previously, excellent knowledge of the law is the code of the category and not a positioning statement. This means that the overall message of a website must convey that the firm is busy in the right areas. The photos used have to be of a quality befitting a law firm's position and convey the right look and feel in a consistent way. Texts have to be confident and relevant, not necessarily fact ridden and detailed. And here is the biggest shock: although individual lawyers have a profile on the website, those are not profile building. A lawyer's website profile simply has to confirm a position. Even so, lawyers have a tendency to spend proportionately more time on their website profile than on actually thinking about how to build their position.

Positioning is the art of operating (and staying) in the segment of the market that a law firm wants to operate in. This has to be done on a very broad front, and it has to be done consciously and consistently for a long period of time. It is the sum of the characteristics that the market ascribes to a firm. A picture emerges, conjured up by all the little bits a law firm and its individuals provide. To be successful at it, a law firm has to live this picture, not just try to look like it.

KEY POINTS

- At a time when large parts of legal work have become a commodity in the eyes of the client, the positioning of a law firm becomes the most important distinguishing factor.

- Most law firms have no clue how to consciously manage their positioning. Herein lies a danger, but because it concerns the vast majority of firms, it does not constitute a great threat. There is, however, a tremendous opportunity for those law firms that come to grips with positioning.
- Many law firms struggle with a realistic view of where they stand. The complexity and uniqueness of their own practices tends to be overestimated.

6

ECCE HOMO

This book is about the need for law firms to change in order to survive. To find the strategy that will take a firm through this process, a law firm first needs to know exactly how it is constructed. A ruthless self-analysis must precede change to have a hope of putting in place a realistic strategy that can actually be achieved. Otherwise, it is just an empty promise leading down a false trail. Just as in the process of charting our human DNA, the same questions are propelling the analysis of a law firm: Who am I? How have I become who I am?

For a law firm, such an analysis starts with the partner group. The dynamics of a firm's partnership is linked to how the partners got there. Where do they come from? Is there a bond between them? Do they have the same culture? Do they *like* each other? Do they trust each other? If a law firm is the product of a merger, whether recent or more than a decade ago, one will nearly always find a thermocline dividing two currents in the partnership. Further, what is the age spread? How long before the senior statesmen will retire, and do they have successors?

The DNA of a firm's partner group depends to a great extent on how the partners came to be part of the group. A *New York Times* article[1] describes how Cravath, Swaine & Moore went about hiring the Obama administration's former top antitrust lawyer, Christine A. Varney, as the fourth outside partner in 50 years. She had to first meet all 83 partners plus any retired partner who wanted to sit down with her. Over two days, she was interviewed by the entire partnership to ensure not whether she would be a good enough lawyer but whether she would be a good Cravath partner. A strongly fused partnership is essential to Cravath's strategy.

Another factor deciding the kinetics of a partnership is cultural background. A firm that sprawls internationally has to look at the different cultural backgrounds of partners and how that background may influence loyalties. Take the partners in the Paris office of an international law firm: will they have a sense of belonging to the firm as a whole or to its Parisian office? Lawyers at multiple locations in one jurisdiction may feel a stronger link to each other than they feel with personnel at the head office on a different continent. This can foster an "us against them" sentiment. Another important factor is, what is the corporate language? Often, it is English, which gives a perceived advantage to native speakers in any internal communication. In many businesses, English as the primary language sows resentment and a perception of bias. The bankers, executives, novelists, thinkers, and politicians who make it internationally mostly have in common the fact that they speak near perfect English. It has been reported that studies in business life have shown that when you speak Globish, the simplest form of English, in an international surrounding, your IQ as perceived by others drops approximately 30 points.[2]

Succession is a fundamental element in the analysis of a law firm. The demands on a partner are vastly different today than they were at the turn of the millennium. They must cope with the reality of a business that has changed and the fact that continuous change demands a different set of tools. We do not pause to contemplate that the partners in year 2000 are to a great extent the same partners as today. A lawyer becomes partner at, say, 35 years of age, give or take a few years. He or she will retire at 60 or even at 70 perhaps. That is a 25- to 35-year period of being a partner. A lot can happen in two and a half decades, and although a person grows with the challenges, the rate of change has sped up. This perspective on partner succession enables us to appreciate the difficulty of the task: How will senior partners of today be able to train the partners of an even more demanding tomorrow?

The importance of proper preparation for tomorrow's partners is often underestimated, and therein lies a danger.

Law firms tend to think of succession as a matter of the right training in terms of technical skills and business awareness. Increasing resources are employed to this end, and MBA institutes across the world are reaping the profits. But there is more to prepping your successors than that. Merely sending junior partners on business training will not ensure a pool of partners ready for succession. This is not how you breed the trusted boardroom advisor. Although some skills of tomorrow's lawyers will be new and different from those possessed by partners made a decade ago, the core qualities remain the same.

Merely sending junior partners on business training will not ensure a pool of partners ready for succession

It can best be explained as two ends of a spectrum, both of which need to be present in a good partner of today. On the one end are technical skills, which have become increasingly demanding. Most prominently, the pace has increased. The speed at which matters were handled two decades ago is not acceptable today. On the other side of the spectrum is what can best be described as personal skills; *how* a good lawyer acts. Effectively solving problems and getting what you want from people is not something that is always defined or explained. The best way to learn these unuttered, subtle yet important personal skills is to observe and copy someone who is better than you. If you want boardroom advisors, then they must have had a chance to access the boardroom and observe how it works. If you want skillful litigators, then young litigators must have had a chance to observe how the seasoned litigator achieves seemingly unattainable outcomes.

One of the best partners I know is the trusted advisor of the boards of several large corporations. He learned his skills as a very young lawyer from two senior partners who were then what he himself is now. He started by literally carrying their bags to and from meetings and, in doing so, could follow them into the places where strategic corporate decisions were made. He had the chance to observe what it is assumed that new partners are just supposed to know: how the most impactful decisions are made. No management training made him into the person whom a chairman phones when a company is about to bet the farm. And yet, the partners who are about to fill his shoes and the shoes of partners like him are left to swim on their own with the silly flotation-aid of a two-week MBA. How is anyone supposed to become a good partner without first having seen what that looks like?

Many of the partners made two decades ago would not have been made partners by today's standards and are not suitable as role models. A well-managed long-term process ensures not only that the successor is ready to fill the shoes of a profitable partner but also that the clients are prepared as well. As argued earlier, the higher up the ranks of complex legal work, the more tied to individuals it becomes. It takes time for clients to transfer such trust to a replacement.

Not many firms have the ability to home-grow every partner. A few law firms can do so successfully because they simply have the role models. Slaugther and May as well as Cravath, Swaine & Moore are two such firms, and the way they make their partners is an integral part of who they are. They are examples of firms who know that the only way to learn how to become a partner is to observe and copy the behavior of existing partners. They can do this because their partners simply have the right level to be duplicated. They can themselves be the best role models, and they use this advantage to create the best training possible. As Cravath states on its website:

> Our partners come from the ranks of our own associates. Our policy is to take the most talented law students and entrust their training only to ourselves. We rotate our associates at all levels of seniority among different partner groups within their department to develop broad expertise in all our practice areas. This combination of natural talent, common training and broad experience produces partners and associates who consistently perform at the very top of the legal profession.[3]

Nearly all law firms rotate their trainees and associates among different partner groups and departments to help them develop broad expertise. But that approach is not going to make partnership candidates unless there are partners whose behavior it is worthwhile to copy.

Most of the legal profession no longer uses this as a succession method. The system in which high-powered partners mentored younger partners or associates to whom they would transfer the bulk of their business when they retired has been abandoned without further thought. It is seen as archaic in this day and age. Making lawyers learn how to become a partner by observing the best is an underestimated and often overlooked ingredient that is key to maintaining a law firm's level.

Whether or not firms are suited to the in-house cultivation of top partners, having partners come only from a law firm's own ranks of associates might not necessarily be the best strategy for firms other than the likes of Slaughter and May or Cravath. In most cases, fresh blood is a good thing. Moreover, the fast-paced adaptability required of today's law firms often leaves lateral hiring as the only way to change within a necessary timeframe.

The so-called Cravath system, developed by Paul D. Cravath, the presiding partner at Cravath, Swaine & Moore from 1906 until his death in 1940, sets collective well-being above individual partners. Individual stars are not allowed to shine at the expense of other partners, presumably because inequality breeds jealousy, which could lead to the demise of the entire partnership. Financial risks and rewards are shared equally. Partners are paid the same lockstep compensation and benefits, the total amount based on seniority. Partners are, with a few exceptions, homegrown so that they are steeped in the firm's culture and traditions. When Cravath hired its 84th partner from outside this system, it did not pay her a signing bonus or give her a guarantee. Cravath is simply paying her according to the firm's seniority-based, lockstep system.

Lateral hires may be what undid Dewey & LeBoeuf, but that does not mean that they cannot be a good thing. If this approach is balanced with the level of a law firm's in-house cultivation of partners, bringing in partners from outside can enforce or launch crucial new practice areas as well as address the festering inefficiencies that come from inbreeding. At the same time, a law firm must demonstrate to associates that it is possible to make it to partnership. If none of the new partners in the past few years have come from within and are instead from talent grown elsewhere, then loyalty and culture will suffer as a result.

At the same time, increased lateral movement has made this a risky business for law firms. Instead of building talent, most law firms buy talent because it is seen as a better bet. The risk that your homegrown successors will be snatched away by a competitor that is offering him or her 25 percent more than what you are offering is very real. Laterally hired partners can be mercenaries with little interest in investing in the law firm as a whole. Their loyalty may last only as long as profits do. This circumstance, of course, is fatal to a partnership culture, except in those law firms that have been built to absorb the shocks of departing partners.

We have seen major lateral partner moves lately, even among firms that historically count on repeat business from loyal A-list clients. It has been reported that even Magic Circle firms have taken steps to prepare for the hire of US partners, such as loosening up their strict lockstep system to accommodate different expectations of remuneration. A review of remuneration systems, for example, by both Linklaters and Freshfields could see the firms looking at ways to better reward strong performers. This could be necessary to attract talent and stay at the top of their game. At the same time, a nonegalitarian remuneration system will not encourage partners to spend their own valuable time in working for the greater good of the firm. Case allocation would be even less accepted, as would other measures aimed at strengthening the position of the firm rather than the profile of the individual partner.

New partners do not necessarily have to be hijacked away from another firm. The top layer of US law firms can benefit from something that is very rare in, for example, Europe. In the United States, there is interplay between talented people in government and law firms. A perfect example is the story of Cravath hiring the president's former top antitrust lawyer. In the same way, partners from influential law firms leave to take top positions within the government and their previous law firm gains a valuable alumnus.

The principle of up or out serves to keep the proportions of different levels of experience, which translates to different hourly rates, balanced in a law firm. If senior associates keep amassing, then a law firm becomes top heavy. Senior associates cost more than junior associates. At the same time, there are partners who thrive with a top-heavy team, and the position of counsel has been created to accommodate senior associates who, for whatever reason, will not become partners. They add considerably to a partner's turnover, and they have almost the same level of expertise, which frees up a lot of time to manage more of them. A partner can leverage himself or herself nicely this way. But having too many lawyers who do not move on is not a good thing. Eventually, many senior practitioners must either become partners or leave the firm. Law firms will be wise to oversee this process carefully because those lawyers will often leave for an in-house position with a client or in the court system. I know a lawyer who was made to leave a law firm because it did not see a future for him within its ranks. The process of ousting him was suboptimal, to say the least. It could have been irrelevant for the law firm had he not gone on to become the general counsel and board member of a global player in the chemical industry and a *Fortune* Global 500 company. He vowed never, ever to work with this law firm again and has held true to his oath. It is shortsighted and ignorant of a law firm not to nurture an alumni network. Many of the world's most successful consultancies are known for their strong alumni networks that function as a silent army of influential people all over the world who help each other and refer work. Research by The Economist Intelligence Unit (EIU) found that informal professional networks and communities are more important for entrepreneurial success than any formal structure.[4] Many successful law firms have the same reverence for their alumni. Recently, I found myself standing in line at an airport next to a partner I knew from many years ago. He had just been spending three days in the Mediterranean taking part in an alumni event of a Global Elite law firm where he had worked briefly as an associate 25 years ago. That is how strong their alumni network is. Some law firms are even using their alumni network as a pool of 'flexible skills' from which people are brought back in as needed, not as associates but as freelancers.

Any strategy for filling a firm's partnership, whether it is the Cravath way or a more nuanced method, starts from the bottom with the recruitment process. Today's lawyer must be more than just excellent at law. A good lawyer has to be creative, solution-driven, immune to stress, worldly wise, and have excellent people skills. A law firm that wants to recruit the talent of the future must first have a vision of what that future might look like and who could fit in it. Do new recruits necessarily have to have an all legal background? Law schools were never good at preparing law students sufficiently for the legal marketplace. This is something taken care of by the law firm itself. But since this is the case, why not consider people with a background that might just make them approach things differently? In England and Wales, a student need not complete four to five years of law studies at university. It is quite common that lawyers have a degree in something other than law, be it languages or English literature. With this qualifying degree, they can complete a conversion course in order to enroll in a legal practice course. Having a bachelor of arts instead of a bachelor of laws degree might have its advantages. Different backgrounds lead to a richer team. If you are above-average smart, you can always learn law. Law schools would not have the overproduction of law graduates that they have if legal studies were suited only to smart people. The scarcity sits in the creative side of legal talent. Law firms and lawyers are increasingly being judged on their ability to innovate, especially in the higher segments. Many law firms have already put in place incentives that will foster and encourage out-of-the-box thinking. The FT Innovative Lawyers report and ranking, based on thorough research on the innovations of law firms and their lawyers carried out by RSG Consulting in partnership with the *Financial Times*, was first released in 2005 and quickly became one of the most prestigious and coveted rankings for lawyers and law firms. During a decade of investigation into innovation in the legal sector, the report has broadened, keeping pace with the increasing demands of the legal profession. The 2015 report looks at the game-changers of the past 10 years and the firms behind the top innovations. There is not one firm that does not want to find itself in this report. Perhaps it is all the more coveted because it is so hard to achieve. Innovation does not come easily to many law firms.

Obvious to most people is that the availability of technology drives the demand for new skills in lawyers. Developments in communication technology have increased the pace of the legal profession. Email has replaced letters, and most lawyers are available on their mobiles 24/7. But aside from the ability to handle stress, other skills that are less often identified are just as essential in response to this change.

For example, the availability of copy-and-paste functions has led to an explosion in the length of lawyers' opinions. Because it requires so little effort, these days many lawyers have the tendency to copy in large pieces of text from other sources for the sake of completeness, whereas lawyers before the copy-and-paste era had to be more selective and summarize much more, using their own words.

How can a profession with the profile of never risking its own money readily agree to try out potentially winning strategies for their own firm if these also run the risk of failure?

The understanding of the DNA of law firms starts with a pivotal question. Why do people become lawyers? A lawyer is someone who, by definition, acts on someone else's behalf. Although the stakes might be high, it is the client who bears the risk of failure. At most, depending on the fee structure, a lawyer will risk his or her compensation if the outcome is unsuccessful. Just like the asset manager of an investment fund, a lawyer typically has no "skin in the game," a phrase coined by investor Warren Buffett, who stands as a symbol of putting his money where his mouth is. I am not saying that this is not as it should be. I am pointing out that it says something about people who choose not to take risks. Lawyers in a business law firm chose the role of being a high-stakes player, but in reality they have little to lose. How can a profession with the profile of never risking its own money readily agree to try out potentially winning strategies for their own firm if these also run the risk of failure?

Recruiters and law firms alike would argue that it would be complex to devise an accurate system of assessing whether a candidate will be a good fit, an innovator and an apt future partner, rather than just a good lawyer. And yet, many recruitment departments at large law firms religiously apply assessment tests to weed out weak people. One element that distinguishes a top lawyer from, let us say, a paralegal, is an above-average ability to read other people. And yet, when it comes to recruiting new talent, surprisingly, law firms turn to such questionable tools as assessment tests. These tests not only testify to an inability to read other people—the recruitment process would look different if it relied on this ability—they also give a false sense of certainty because people behave differently in the artificial setting of a test. Test results often do not match reality. One might also question whether someone with a strong character would agree to participate in such an assessment test or even apply in the first place. Some law firms have realized that the odds are stacked against the fostering of new skills and are trying to put systems in place to encourage skills in addition to mere diligence and knowledge of the law. In 2013, it was reported that conclusions based on feedback from associates within Slaughter and May recommended a more merit-based pay arrangement.[5] The firm went on to revamp its appraisal system and now issues higher remuneration to associates who show outstanding performance in areas other than legal skills, including business and communications skills, practice management skills, and people skills.

At one point in time, I was present at a law firm management team meeting. A last-minute topic had been added to the agenda that first needed to be dealt with. Two young associates had come to one of the practice heads in tears because they had had a verbal berating from one of the partners. A legal piece they had produced was, in the partner's view, below par and would have to be redone before anyone left for home. Sharp words fell that elaborated on the partner's opinion about the intellectual capacities of the two young associates. The members of the management team immediately took to discussing how they should address this lashing out with the partner in question on the basis that it is unacceptable to make your associates cry. This knee-jerk reaction illustrates the tendency to coddle young lawyers that has gradually seeped in from other industries and now permeates law firms too. My advice in this scenario would not be to tap the partner on the fingers but to fire the two associates—not because they had produced unacceptable work but because they had cried. The verbal lashing they had received had been kept on a professional level, not a personal one. If that brings someone to tears, then that person is better suited to working elsewhere. Being a lawyer at the level of the firm that these two associates worked at takes an inner robustness and a readiness to fight. Nobody is forcing anyone to work in the top level of the legal profession. Just being good at law does not make you suited to work in the field. As the old saying goes, if you cannot stand the heat, get out of the kitchen. There is a business model to fit every attitude. But the combination of attitude and the strategy of a law firm need to be right. Shedding tears is not conducive to operating in a business law firm. The combination of a law firm in a noncommoditized segment of the legal market and emotional pampering is not a good one.

The tendency to coddle young lawyers has gradually seeped in from other industries and now permeates law firms too

Somehow, the homegrown monster of the HR department has been allowed to take over. Theories about the employee and the workforce are wielded as if they were of academic stature. There are company psychologists who specialize in employability and social innovation. Out comes the holistic approach to an employee: it becomes the employer's task to care for the person as a whole. Training (and they love training) should be not only on work content but also on personal development. This culture grows uncurbed because who is openly going to oppose the values attached to being a good employer? But law firms were not consulted when these values were established. As a result, the pampering is counteracting efforts to get lawyers into suitable shape to become partners. In most law firms these days, HR plays an integral role not only in picking the recruits but also in selecting the ones who make associates. The lawyers involved in this process tend to purely focus on the legal skills of the candidates because that is all they feel competent to judge. The process of hiring and fostering the right skills to have as a lawyer is a vital part of the very strategy of a law firm. It should be drawn up at the highest level, implemented in the most suitable way, and painstakingly monitored. Caring about your employees is about striking a balance. To propagate a system like the one that drove a summer intern in 2014 at the London city office of a US bank to commit suicide is not only inhumane and arrogant but also foolish and counter to what any business would want to achieve. A system that promotes people who stand up for themselves needs to reward that very quality. This is not done by being persuaded by tears but by being open to well-argued solutions, even if they tend to be worked out in overtime.

That leads me to kill off another hobby horse that has entered with the HR industry: work–life balance. Like I said, nobody is forced to work at the top level of the law or at any other level for that matter. If you do, it comes at a price. The difference in practicing a sport at an amateur level and making a stab at the professional level is immense. It comes with many sacrifices. The notion that you can enter the ranks of legal practitioners at the top of their game, earn a million dollars or more per year, and still go home at five o'clock every day is preposterous. And yet, this is an attitude frequently encountered. Many of the young lawyers today may have been brought up with the notion that such levels of commitment are made only for your own start-up. At the same time, HR plays into the hands of such attitudes, leading the new generation to believe that they have the right to not pay too high a price for work performed for someone else.

The notion that you can enter the ranks of lawyers at the top of their game, earn a million dollars or more per year, and still go home at five o'clock every day is preposterous

In 2020, millennials will be representing a full 40 percent of the total working population in the United States, according to the Intelligence Group, the publisher of an ongoing cultural study of young consumers (the *Cassandra Report*).[6] The millennials, or Generation Y, are members of the generation with birth years ranging from the early 1980s to the early 2000s, although there are no precise dates marking when the generation starts and ends. Generation X, the generation preceding the millennials, seems to be sentenced to finding their younger siblings flighty and unwilling to pay their dues. Generation X is the generation born after the western post–World War II baby boom, with birth dates ranging from the early 1960s to the early 1980s. Some researchers have attributed the restlessness of the millennials to the generation's attitude toward work: work is something you do to be part of changing things for the better, not just to earn a living. The Intelligence Group claims that, according to its survey, 72 percent of the millennials would like to be their own boss. But if they do have to work for a boss, 79 percent of them would want that boss to serve more as a coach or mentor.

Eighty-eight percent prefer a collaborative work culture. *Forbes* published an interview with the chief strategy officer for the Intelligence Group in which he explains that millennials are, in essence, "venture consumers."[7] They are not looking to fill a slot in a faceless company. Instead, they are looking at opportunities to invest strategically in a place where they can make a difference and be part of something that has an impact. Maybe prestige and money are not the top two drivers anymore in the legal profession—maybe it is about buy-in. Whatever the answer is to what triggers the new generation, for a law firm it comes down to the same: in order to recruit the talent of the future, you must first have a vision of that future looks like and who fits in it. Doing so, and doing so well, is a way of implementing a law firm's strategy and crucial to its long-term survival.

I am deeply convinced that a multicultural environment and differences among people are good and lead to the best results. A homogenous group will not be an innovative group, and it will not likely adapt well to change. All law firms pay lip service to diversification and many of them also put words into action. Unfortunately, often in these cases, the representatives of diversity (they can usually be counted on the fingers of one hand) are set up to fail.

For example, if a firm has a strong culture based on a specific sociological background, then an outsider will always feel like an outsider. Unwritten codes, the particular sense of humor, and many other little details will effectively isolate them. Nobody wants to be somewhere for the sake of statistics. It also takes a very strong mind to go through all the incidents of having to be the poster face of a firm. I know of a case where an associate was the only representative of a minority and had to put up with always being asked to participate in pictures. It was demeaning, and he left for a younger, more diverse law firm.

Having attended countless lawyer conferences all over the world, I know there is always one session devoted to diversity. Especially in the United States, where clients demand more reporting on diversity, there is always an entry on the program for a slot dedicated to being politically correct. I have made a point of looking around the room, usually filled with at least 200 lawyers, when the diversity agenda point is being discussed in order to try to estimate the percentage of diversity.

Without exception, it comes up shockingly short. Often, there is no sign of diversity at all as I find myself in a room with all white males from well-to-do backgrounds.

When I first went to Africa, I noted that a surprisingly large percentage of lawyers and businesspeople I met there were women. Among western law firms, female partners are still—to varying degrees—being used as poster faces. Not being serious about diversity is a missed opportunity and a waste of talent. Intense cooperation in teams with both genders and backgrounds from all over the world, in my experience, always leads to innovation and new insights, especially when the clients they want to serve are as diverse—and more and more of them are.

KEY POINTS

- Demands on partners have dramatically increased over the past decade or so. As a consequence, some of the longer-sitting partners would not have been made partner today.
- Growing the next generation of partners might require skills that the past generation does not have. At the same time, the new generation needs to learn by observing and copying the successful partners of today.
- Lateral hires are a way of overcoming this obstacle. This practice has led to increased partner mobility.
- Diversity in cultural background brings challenges, but it drives change and innovation.
- Being a lawyer, and subsequently being a partner in a business law firm, is in many ways comparable to competing in the Olympic Games. Playing in the top league comes at a price. Those who are not willing to pay the price should look for employment elsewhere rather than being led to believe that there is a way to both have the cake and eat it.

7

THE FINANCIAL MODEL

It is necessary to understand a few basic calculations in order to understand the profit model of a law firm. They are deceptive in their simplicity and yet fundamental to how a law firm operates. On the basic level of a law firm, the following straightforward formula describes how profit is calculated:

Turnover – Cost = Profit = 0

The cost of the law firm is subtracted from the turnover achieved every year. Left over is the profit of that year, which is distributed in full among the equity partners in accordance with either the lockstep system or the "eat what you kill" method. At the end of each year, there is zero cash left in the firm. It is important to understand that the cost is almost entirely fixed. I will elaborate on the consequences of this later.

The lockstep method of dividing the firm's profit comes with some inherent consequences. Every partner receives a share of the profit based on points. These points are accrued in steps based on seniority and a few other criteria that have been defined by the partnership. Say that a partner starts with 40 points. Every year, he or she earns extra points based on a predetermined scale. A partner reaches the maximum of 100 points relatively quickly. The profit is divided among the equity partners as follows: first you divide the profit by the total number of points that are held by the partners.

$$\frac{\textbf{Profit}}{\Sigma \textbf{ All the points of the equity partners}}$$

This calculation establishes what each point is worth, that is, the value per point, for that year. Each partner subsequently receives the sum of his or her points times the value per point. It can be illustrated with a simple example.

There are five partners, and their points are as follows: partner 1 has 40 points, partner 2 and partner 3 each have 100 points, partner 4 has 60 points, and partner 5 has 75 points. This makes a total of 375 points. If the profit that year is $10 million, then the value per point is $10 million divided by 375. This produces a number of 0.02666 per point. Each partner receives the sum of his or her points multiplied by 0.02666:

P1: 40 × 0.02666 = $1.066 million
P2: 100 × 0.02666 = $2.666 million
P3: 100 × 0.02666 = $2.666 million
P4: 60 × 0.02666 = $1.599 million
P5: 75 × 0.02666 = $1.999 million

This point system has a crucial consequence. If the turnover stays the same and the costs stay the same, then the value per point will keep going down as equity partners automatically earn their lockstep points. If the pie stays the same, the slices will become smaller, as you need to cut more of them. Unless a law firm increases its profit every year, the partners with 100 points will see their profit per equity partner (PEP) dwindle each year.

The way a law firm distributes its profit each year also has consequences. Partners are suspicious by nature. "Each one for himself and God for us all" is the prevailing motto. By distributing all profit, every year, each partner will reap the benefits immediately rather than risking that it is all gone by tomorrow. This means that a law firm will not build up a capital buffer for investments. For most law firms, each investment must be carried by each year's expected profits. Each partner will estimate whether he or she will ever benefit from the return on the investment and vote accordingly. Toward the end of their service, partners may not take a long-term view. This is also in part why banks are reluctant to lend to law firms. There is a high level of unpredictability in the cash flow, and there are few secure assets to lend against. Even the future stream of income is often not bankable because clients seldom guarantee any turnover. There are no contracts to securitize. Notwithstanding the reluctance of banks to lend to law firms, the *Financial Times* reported in 2015 that bank lending to law firms in the United Kingdom had increased by 28 percent since 2010.[1] Technology improvements and funding expansion have been cited by the law firms as targets for investment in the coming years.

Unless a law firm increases its profits every year, the partners with 100 points will see their PEP dwindle each year

Crucial to comprehending the profit model of a law firm is understanding its costs. The costs are more or less all fixed. There are no raw materials or products with fluctuating prices that a law firm needs to buy in large quantities. There is no expensive equipment that it needs to maintain and update. The variables are mostly nonbillable expenses, training, temporary employees, and office supplies. As variable costs go, all of these are relatively steady and foreseeable. The largest part of a law firm's cost, around 60 percent, comprises the fixed costs in the form of salaries for the nonequity fee earners and staff. The rest of the cost consists of costs for offices, which are also fixed costs. The cost percentage of the revenue is roughly between 60 and 70 percent. Out of a $100 turnover, an average of $65 will go to covering costs. It is important to realize that these costs are predominantly fixed. This has consequences for how a law firm must think about profit. A law firm that wants to look at how it can best increase its profits in a sustainable way must examine what measures it can take to increase turnover and to reduce costs. How can the number of hours worked be increased? How can we price smarter? Where is profit leaking away? Which costs can be sliced?

One of the most obvious profit eaters is the discount that partners often too readily give away. Lawyers often underestimate the impact that discounts have on profit. The simple and direct relationship between turnover, cost, and profit means that the discounts that partners tend to give on their hourly rate have a multiplied impact on the firm's profits simply because the costs are fixed. For example, turnover is made up of billable hours. If we have one billable hour of $100, and the fixed cost is $65 per $100, then we have $35 as profit for each billable hour. If a partner gives a 5 percent discount on the hourly rate, then this is a $5 loss of turnover. But since the costs are fixed, it means that it is also immediately a $5 loss of profit. Reducing $35 by $5 represents a decrease of 14.3 percent. Thus, a 5 percent discount on the turnover translates into a 14.3 percent loss of profit. Often, even partners do not realize this relationship between deduction on price and reduction of profit as they casually agree to discounts.

Often, even partners do not realize the relationship between deduction on price and reduction of profit as they casually agree to discounts

Law firms of all sizes write off or write down a large amount of time. This practice used to be so common that it was considered simply part of providing legal services. As the crisis hit and pricing has come under pressure, write-offs have come increasingly under the magnifying glass of law firms. They are usually attributed to poor communication with the client and weak case management, but there are often more reasons than that. There are two categories of write-offs: those done before the invoice is drawn up and those done after the invoice has been sent. The second category usually comes down to poor communication with a client where expectations were not clearly formulated from the start and expectation management along the way was lacking. Before clients started to take control of the procurement of legal services and alternative fee arrangements (AFAs) entered the legal market, forcing law firms to work on their planning skills, price adjustments tended largely to be a post mortem matter, so to speak. Law firms went about their business, as they have done for decades, and billed all hours worked until a client complained, at which point the invoice was adjusted accordingly. Many clients routinely ask for a reduction of the bill once they receive it and get 10 percent without any further ado. If a client feels it really has a cause for complaint, the reduction will increase. Although lawyers still by nature have a tendency to offer a discount at the drop of a hat, it is now much more a case of prior agreement before any invoice is drawn up.

The category of write-offs made before the invoice is drawn up is often the result of bad case management. This refers to file management at partner level and should not be confused with project management, which is a technical aid. Often, associates spend too much time performing legal work, either because they are being pressed to maximize billable hours or because they are not given clear instructions or clear time restrictions. However, one of the most significant culprits when it comes to working excessive hours is colleague partners who are called in to provide specialized support on other partner's files. They tend not to feel the pressure of the client and have no overview of the matter as a whole, which makes them less cautious in how they spend their hours. The worst kinds of hours that cannot be invoiced, however, are the ones that are never written down in the first place. Sometimes these work as a stealth discount. Due to loyalties in referral relationships, a price is agreed upon, often through the mere mention of it by the dominant referring party. The partner handling the referral work can keep his or her hourly rate—or value, as it were—intact, but by not writing down a certain number of hours, he or she will arrive at the agreed or expected amount every time. In return, the partner will receive a next referral, and so on, and his or her desk is less likely to be empty. This kind of write-off means a law firm has no overview of where or how much profit is leaking away.

A basic cash flow management motto is to bill quickly and chase for payment promptly if required. This is also key for the turnover. Surprisingly, monthly invoicing is an exception rather than a rule within law firms. Lawyers are often too busy to write down their hours on a daily basis. Those days can turn into weeks. Before an invoice can be sent out covering a certain period, all team members must have written in their hours. This is why clients can be heard complaining about lawyers' bills not being timely. They seldom are. Once the lawyers get around to it, the invoice may have accumulated so many hours that an extraordinary sum arrives on the desk of the client. The *Wall Street Journal* reported that after the collapse of Howrey, the ensuing lawsuits showed that Howrey, in the year before its collapse, was taking inventive measures to persuade partners to collect on unpaid legal bills. The firm formed a "Hall of Shame" for partners whose uncollected bills topped $150,000 and were more than 120 days past due. About 35 partners were initially inducted into the Hall of Shame in early 2010, and the list grew until the firm was dissolved in 2011.[2]

Lawyers usually perceive good client relationships and recoveries to be at odds with one another. Partners often hesitate to follow up on fees that have not been paid because they anticipate a probable conflict that may negatively affect their relationship with the client. Partners are often not even aware of the monthly progress on invoicing and collections, and there is often no culture of calling upon them personally to review and ensure fees are collected. This is a situation that peer pressure in the partnership should keep under control rather than leaving it to a financial manager.

In the financial model of a law firm, everyone needs to make his or her hours. It is still the measure by which law firms plan. Billable hours can easily be quantified and kept for historical reference and serve as a guide for lawyers' performances and evaluations. The time sheet that law firms meticulously fill out to produce an invoice at the end of the month is also the "inventory" of a law firm. The calculation of a law firm's budget for the coming year is quite basic: take the number of associates and multiply it by the target number of hours, and then make a small correction per practice group based on current cases and expectations of the market for the coming year. Out comes a number that can be used when planning expenses that have to be accommodated that year. But, as we all know, a year can turn out differently than expected.

A law firm would be wise to analyze precisely where any increase in turnover comes from. As demonstrated, a small increase in turnover will have an immediate effect on profit. But if this relatively small increase in turnover comes from an upward adjustment of rates, then the increase is not the result of the firm performing better. In fact, such an increase can help to hide the fact that the firm is actually doing worse. A better indicator for how a law firm is doing is the number of billable and recovered hours. The elementary relationship between turnover, fixed costs, and profit means that any small increase in revenue creates a larger increase in profits percentage wise. Or, put differently, any increase in turnover is money straight in the bank. There is a target number of billable hours per year per fee earner. If the average amount is 6 billable hours per day per fee earner, and each fee earner surpasses this target by 15 minutes each day, this translates into a 10 to 13 percent higher profit if using a fixed cost of 60 to 70 percent. The opposite is also true. A small decrease in the billable hours leads to a proportionately larger decrease in profits. Again, this is because costs remain fixed. There is, of course, a limit to how much extra work a law firm can do with the same number of people.

As a general rule, fee earners are expected to bill three times their salary. This will cover the cost of their own salary, their share in the firm's overhead, and the partners' profits. A partner's own billable hours will not make the necessary profit. This is often a trap that partners fall into. When work is running low, they carry out an increasing share of the work personally in order to reach their own hourly target. This is a mistake. In a traditional law firm, model associates earn the profit. Apart from that, by hoarding the work, a partner will be doing work that would normally be delegated to a lower competency level, which often means higher write-offs to keep clients satisfied. Such partners are also less busy maintaining competence level among associates. It used to be doctrine that law firm profitability depended heavily on leveraging a high ratio of associates to partners. But this gospel has changed with the commoditization of law. Leverage has become a measure of commoditization. The old idea that the more associates who can be kept busy, the higher the profit is no longer true. The type of work that can keep high numbers of associates busy is low-level work, and this work simply carries a much lower price tag. Just like milk in the supermarket, a law firm will have to sell large volumes to make its margins. High revenues often come paired with

Leverage has become a measure of commoditization

lower profits per partner. In the AmLaw 100, based on the figures of 2015, none of the top 10 firms in terms of PEP, except for Kirkland & Ellis, are in the top 10 firms ranked on turnover.

It is clear that high leverage is not necessarily what will bring profits to equity partners. As explained, there is an optimum composition of a team working on a case. Using more of the most profitable level of associates, without compromising on the quality of work, can significantly increase the profit per partner. But the type of work will dictate what level of associates, and how many, can be used. Different practices have different ratios of associates to partners. During the recession, many firms reduced their associate ranks—and even now, many are still hiring fewer new associates than they used to. Increased outsourcing, flexible skills, maximized internal efficiencies, and even software have contributed to maintaining or even lowering leverage in comparison to where it was just before the crisis.

The American Lawyer is a monthly law magazine published by ALM. Globally, lawyers look to the annual AmLaw 100 and AmLaw 200 surveys that this magazine conducts, which rank law firms by number of attorneys, profits per partner, and overall revenue. The data is based on voluntary reporting from the firms. US law firms are more willing than firms in other countries to report their numbers, including their profit. The purely European equivalent of AmLaw 100 is the Lawyer European 100, ranking the top 100 independent firms on the continent by turnover. These market intelligence reports fill a vital function for law firms, since referring to them is one of the easiest ways to benchmark themselves against competitors.

Due to the lockstep point system, there is always a spread between the partners who pull in most of the turnover and the partners who contribute the least amount of turnover. On average, the relationship between the highest and lowest earning partner is three to one. The highest-earning partner will tend to complain about the least successful partners. Sometimes, law firms feel they have no choice but to accommodate such dissatisfaction by punishing the lowest-grossing partners by reducing their points. In a so-called managed lockstep, this is done more easily. When some of the points of a poorly performing partner are canceled, he or she will receive less in the annual share of profit. There may even be built in gateways at one or two places on the lockstep through which a partner will pass only if the firm agrees that he or she should progress further. However, for most firms, a penalty system of point reduction is a bad measure because it does not lead to a solution. A partner with fewer points will simply lose the incentive to work harder. A stick is only effective as a deterrent. Reducing the points once someone has performed poorly only serves to legitimize the fact that such a partner can stop trying altogether. In the end, such a law firm will be left with an oversized gallery of losers. The only real stick is, "Do better or leave." However, every law firm must accept a number of partners who bring in less profit than the cut they take. It is simply part of the business model. It can be likened to supermarkets that run their business with the measure of profit per square foot. This means that large and cheap goods are the least profitable. If such goods move fast, like milk, then it is okay. However, products such as sugar will remain minimal in profit and sometimes even be unprofitable. At the same time, each supermarket knows that it has to offer sugar to its customers. The cost of offering sugar has to be carried by the more profitable goods. Many law firms have to offer the equivalent of sugar in the supermarket, and the more profitable partners must bear it for the good of the whole partnership.

> *Every law firm must accept a number of partners who bring in less profit than the cut they take. It is simply part of the business model*

It is said that lockstep culture encourages teamwork and collaboration because the profit is shared. However, law firms, notably members of the Magic Circle, have tinkered lately with the strict point system of the lockstep. In their case, it is in preparation of accommodating young partner talent that they want to get on board mainly from the United States. Global expansion is difficult within a strict lockstep system. New talent can receive only the prescribed number of points and will, through little else than seniority, have to work themselves up. This is hardly how you lure talent. Clifford Chance voted through changes to this system in May 2015 that will introduce "super points" for top-performing partners. Freshfields and Linklaters have also suggested that the lockstep may no longer sustain the US partners boosting its New York and Washington, DC, offices.

As shown in previous chapters, AFAs have made their entry and are here to stay. This is not necessarily bad for a law firm's financial model. There are opportunities here, but it does mean that some adjustments have to be made. Doing well with AFAs implies access to as near real-time case management as you can possibly get. Increasingly relying on such a seemingly simple alternative arrangement such as a blended rate means that a law firm needs to know at every point in time what the revenue would be under a normal pricing arrangement. If this is more than the revenue of the blended rate, then the law firm is bleeding profit.

Since profitability is tied to the individual fee earners, a law firm needs to know exactly who is working and when. Any lawyer whose normal rate would be above the blended rate must do only what is absolutely necessary. Every lawyer below the blended rate will make the firm money. There is always an ideal composition of a team for every file. The gap between cost and revenue, which translates into profit, is not the same for every level of associate. Some levels are simply more profitable because they come with less cost relative to the hourly rate they can charge. Smart case management will find this sweet spot for each case.

Most law firms are surprisingly unsophisticated in their method of getting to a fixed price. Not only that, they use only historical data in reaching an estimate

The most difficult AFA to manage is fixed price. Finding and agreeing to a realistic fixed price is a challenge. Most law firms are surprisingly unsophisticated in how they get to a fixed price. Not only that, they use only historical data in reaching an estimate. This is also the biggest pitfall of project management. Project management is a technical process, aided by software, that is increasingly brought in to ensure the success of AFAs. However, the software that forecasts budget overruns and keeps track of pre-agreed milestones is built on historical data only. It merely extrapolates on what was true yesterday.

External factors, not based on historical data, have the largest impact and will be the undoing of a case. Two cases are rarely alike, even if it is commodity work. There is no such thing as the average merger. No two clients are alike. Successful project management must take into account external factors. But creating such software and IT tools is beyond the scope of what lawyers and programmers can at present achieve together. It would take an experienced law firm practitioner with an understanding of algorithms and programming. Until then, law firms will bake an insurance premium into their fixed price, as it will simply be too risky to get many of their fixed price mandates wrong.

Automation in itself can bring costs down. There are certainly advantages to be reaped here. Technology will be part of the answer to commoditization. Computers with smart software will make work more efficient and can take over some of the commodity work that would be unprofitable if done by people due to the pressed price for commodity work. Any increase in capability without taking on extra associates is pure profit. On the other hand, the fact that software can be used means that we are talking about highly commoditized work, which comes with its own set of dilemmas. It must fit the law firm's position and not affect perceptions of the other services offered. Prices are being pressed for commoditized work, and so the volumes need to be larger and the pricing different than the hourly rate.

The ways to bring down costs are often focused on the largest part of them: the salaries. Associates cost money. When there is not enough work to have them earn money or at least carry their own weight, law firms tend to let them go. Traditionally, this measure has been the only flexibility in difficult times. After the 2008 crisis, law firms brought down the number of associates, but many of them came to regret this downsizing bitterly. Letting go of associates is easy, but getting them back, especially the talented ones, is difficult. Years of training have gone down the drain. Some law firms have taken to installing a pool of flexible skill that makes use of their alumni network. DLA Piper teamed up with Lawyers On Demand to help manage a group of flexible lawyers comprised of alumni and other lawyers having worked for the firm. Allen & Overy launched Peerpoint, a business with access to experienced lawyers available to work flexibly for the firm on a contract basis. Simply put, it is an address book of skilled lawyers who want to freelance, providing increased flexibility in meeting peaks in demand. Initially, Peerpoint contracted Allen & Overy alumni, but it also looks to engage lawyers from other firms who are seeking greater flexibility. Flexible skills is not a model these firms use for commodity work. There would be little point in going through all that trouble if the firm could not leverage its strengths and add capacity to noncommoditized or high-end commoditized work. This way, it adds to the profit without harming a firm's position. For the necessary commodity work, higher-tier firms will use outsourcing, nearshoring, or a differently branded technology-driven service.

In microeconomics, bringing down the cost of each unit sold by increasing the scale of operation and thereby spreading fixed costs over more units of output is referred to as *economies of scale*. In the world of law firms, however, there are limits on the cost benefits that can be derived from just being large. Beyond a certain size, economies of scale have their limitations in an industry that is largely reliant on the hourly billing model. If you want to add profit, you need to add hours, and in order to add hours, you need to add people.

Large firms with multiple offices across jurisdictions are much more difficult to manage than smaller firms. Large firms require a much higher investment of resources to achieve uniformity in quality and service delivery and to meet the expectations of clients for efficiency, predictability, and cost effectiveness. They also face unique challenges in maintaining collegial and collaborative cultures, particularly in the face of rapid growth resulting from mergers or large-scale lateral acquisitions. The conflicts of interest also increase. Examples of all these things can be found among the stories of the failed law firms in Chapter 1, "Icarus's Fall."

Having said all this, ways of cutting costs only available to larger firms have gained momentum and sophistication in recent years. Data on alternative sourcing arrangements such as outsourcing, offshoring, and nearshoring suggest that firms can make large savings by using legal, paralegal, and business services capacity in locations away from expensive financial centers. The option of cutting costs in this way is only really available to larger firms. It would hardly be profitable for a small firm to outsource the work of a few people. In the United Kingdom, the cost saving of shifting work from the City to Wales or Northern England represents 60 percent. Large London law firms are sending work to subcontracted law firms in regional centers that have large paralegal teams. Ashurst launched its own low-cost support base in Glasgow a few years ago and has managed to cut its out-of-hours support staff base in London by 120 jobs. Herbert Smith set up a Belfast operation in 2010 to handle volume dispute resolution work. Allen & Overy and Baker & McKenzie have also outsourced some of their back-office functions to Belfast. White & Case outsourced its back-office operations to India a decade ago and within five years opened a center in the Philippines that now covers functions including billing support, financial analysis, conflict support, after-hours reception services and business development.

Other outside-the-firm components that large firms use to replace leverage include legal research and legal process companies, document management firms, and software-as-a-service (SaaS) content providers. The examples are numerous. There is an advantage to firms in jurisdictions whose language is spread beyond its borders. US firms are also outsourcing, although this tends to be more clad in mist, as they decline to report on whether they are outsourcing legal processes. A wall of silence might exist because outsourcing is more sensitive in the United States. English-speaking firms have many more options when it comes to outsourcing, as do those who operate in French and Spanish. French firms have been outsourcing to Francophone Africa for some time.

Other surprising alternatives for European firms closer to home, and with far better connectivity, are emerging. Romania is a case in point: 20 percent of its population speaks French at a high level. A pioneering group of French companies structured the French economic presence in Romania, and it has been growing ever since. Southern Poland, the Czech Republic, and Hungary are also being eyed for future offshore bases by firms around Europe.

Having an office in another jurisdiction is a large cost for a law firm. Often, national champions opt to open supporting offices in other jurisdictions to facilitate transactions across time zones and cultures in order to keep up with the IBL firms. Such a supporting office in most cases will not generate enough turnover to cover the cost of running it. The lawyers are paid on expat terms that often include an allowance for the expatriation of families. The partners working there rarely have a workload that can produce the target number of hours, not to mention the considerably lower leverage due to a lack of associates. Choosing to recruit locally is a risk for such a law firm. Partners with a different background and different loyalties may start running their own show. The best way to control such outposts of your brand is to have trusted guardians in place from among your own partnership. An office abroad also means taking on currency risk. The level of the billing rates also fluctuates across jurisdictions and markets. Local firms experience this effect through the inflated rates often carried by an international deal. The management intensity, operational complexity, and cost of maintaining an office in another country requires that there be a clear path to profit contribution unless a firm can afford to create international allure as a marketing exercise.

The management of a law firm comes with a price tag, just as in any business. The one or two managing partners will not contribute notably to the turnover, since they will not make their hours, while they keep their points—usually the maximum number—and thus their share of the profit. Few partners lament this principle because it leads to fair compensation for their managerial duties. However, management comes with a hidden loss of profit beyond the loss of hours accrued during the managing partner's term. Choosing a managing partner entails a dilemma. On the one hand, a law firm wants to appoint a heavy hitter who carries clout. A profitable partner in the lead is also likely to have more influence in the partnership and can help gain traction when taking the firm forward. On the other hand, the firm risks losing a profitable partner altogether. It is the curse of managing partners that they nearly always lose their practice during the four- to eight-year term. In that period, clients will have migrated to other partners or firms. Often, a former managing partner will have to start over again rather than picking up where he or she left off. For many, this proves unachievable, and within a few years they leave for positions in financial institutions or in-house legal advisory, or they open their own consultancy. Every lawyer can surely think of a number of examples where this has happened.

In the end, due to how the earning model of a law firm is structured, it revolves around the quest for making the gap between turnover and cost as large as possible. This has to be done in a sustainable way, as annual profit must be trumped each year.

KEY POINTS

- In a law firm, costs are predominantly fixed and can, in the short term, only marginally be influenced.
- All turnover minus cost is profit and is distributed in full among partners. A law firm has no savings.
- Given the constant nature of the costs, any decrease in turnover will have a leveraged impact on profit by a typical multiple of three. This means that a 10 percent drop in turnover will constitute a 30 percent drop in profit.
- Even among partners there is insufficient awareness of the consequences this leveraged effect may have.

8

THE ENEMY WITHIN

In the 1970s, the United Kingdom suffered a series of severe strikes by powerful trade unions that led to power cuts, closures of power stations, and industrial disruption. The country was at this time referred to as the "sick man of Europe" by critics of its government at home because of a troubled economy compared to other European countries. The industrial strife and poor economic performance culminated in the Winter of Discontent in 1978–79. After two toppled governments and a bout of unusually hard-hitting strikes, leaving schools closed and hospitals in danger, Margaret Thatcher came to power in 1979. In her first years in office, she was faced with the cold war, the Falklands War, as well as severe clashes with trade unions.

It was against this background that she wrote a highly controversial speech that she was going to deliver for the first time in public at the 1984 conservative party conference in Brighton. In this speech, she planned to state that it was not so much external forces that were a threat to the United Kingdom as it was the undermining by the enemy within. Mrs. Thatcher had been forced to deal with tumultuous global politics where nuclear arms raised the stakes. At the same time, domestic politics meant dealing with challenging economic times characterized by high unemployment and stagnating manufacturing output, with strong unions opposing legislation. If having to prioritize between the external enemies and the enemy within the United Kingdom's own borders, Mrs. Thatcher had made her choice. It would have been a powerful speech that accused not only the militant miners but also the Labour party of being part of an insurrection against democracy. She had spotted what, in her mind, was a far greater stumbling block on the way to prosperity than any external enemy. She was going to point out that the internal disruptor is the greatest threat and that the deadliest blow would come from the enemy within. Mrs. Thatcher's own handwritten notes for the speech were released for the first time by the Margaret Thatcher Foundation in October 2014. "Since Office. Enemy without—beaten him & resolute strong in defence. Enemy within—Miners' leaders . . . Liverpool and some local authorities—just as dangerous . . . in a way more difficult to fight . . . just as dangerous to liberty."[1] The speech was never delivered in public due to the IRA bomb that exploded in the Grand Hotel in Brighton not long before the speech was scheduled.

Partners tend to look for enemies among external competitors, while it is the firm's core mechanism that is the true enemy

There are many parallels to be drawn between politics and the internal workings of a law firm. In many ways, the internal disruptors in a law firm are far more dangerous than any external competition. Partners tend to look for enemies among external competitors, while it is the firm's core mechanism that is the true enemy. To understand the inner workings of a law firm, based on the partnership of its owners, we must understand a few common character traits among lawyers.

The first one is their attention to detail. This sounds obvious, but people tend to underestimate its consequences. A lawyer is someone who is trained to spot inconsistencies and weaknesses in arguments. All day, every day, lawyers are busy finding flaws in the work of others as well as in their own work. They approach every argument and written piece with the assumption that "this cannot be good" in order to rectify any error or find a weak spot to attack. The opposing party also has a lawyer doing the same thing. Day in and day out, a lawyer argues against something. Perseverance is part of this search for details—a refusal to take no for an answer when you need a yes. It is also a question of thoroughness in an area that is difficult to quantify. How does a lawyer know there is no more information he or she can use? When doing legal research, how can a lawyer ever know if he or she has unearthed every possible regulation or case that could have a bearing on the question at hand? If a lawyer is searching out the facts in a high-stakes litigation case, how many stones must be looked under until it can be said that none have been left unturned? The answer is blowing in the wind, because you can never prove a negative. Given enough time, a lawyer can always be a little bit more prepared. A comma in the wrong place in a contract can have a devastating effect, so it must be found and corrected. Any possible risk or exposure hiding in a lawyer's work must be excluded. This focus on details colors everything a lawyer does and how he or she operates. It is part of a lawyer's personality. A person who does not have this character trait simply will not become a lawyer.

The second character trait common among lawyers is one that is seldom brought to attention: insecurity. At the core, lawyers are their own worst critics, driven by a nagging feeling that they are not good enough. Self-doubt can spur many people on to greatness. A continuous evaluation of everything you do—"Have I missed anything?"—can drive a person to be thorough and exacting. This thoroughness is essential. Insecurity is connected to risk aversion and manifests as a focus on detail. An overconfident person will not last very long as a lawyer, and a sloppy person will probably not even want to enter the legal profession to start with. But this perpetual measuring cannot be selectively applied. A lawyer will doubt not only himself or herself when composing a legal opinion but also everything else he or she does professionally. With high hourly tariffs comes the constant self-evaluation: "Am I worth it?" Lawyers have a constant fear of being unmasked by colleagues as untalented. The self-criticism increases the less familiar the lawyer is with a subject, and the realms of law firm management are such unchartered territory that opinions are seldom shared for fear of coming across as stupid.

We often come across the opinion that lawyers are arrogant. Perhaps it is a result of the seriousness a lawyer must portray and the distance he or she needs to maintain to achieve this distance. Familiarity breeds contempt, and to be disrespected is not good for a lawyer. Sometimes, though, that reputation is fueled by occasional prima donna behavior by lawyers. This behavior is not due to perceived superiority or arrogance, however. It stems from an inherent uncertainty or insecurity that leads to overcompensating behavior, much like the behavior of the school bully. If you make yourself as large as possible, then others are less likely to question your invulnerability. Respect has to be demanded, not asked for politely. Lawyers in a law firm, and especially its partners, operate in a highly hierarchical environment. The higher up the ladder you are, the more you have a say in matters concerning your law firm. Keeping that position in the wolf pack means you will occasionally have to bite inferior members.

The third factor to take into account when looking at the behavior of partners in a law firm is their paramount fear of being ousted. This feeling of danger is intensified when a partner's turnover is decreasing, his or her work is becoming less spectacular, power struggles rage, or his or her practice is marginalized through strategy changes. Connected to the central driver of insecurity is the concern of being the next one to be made to leave, and this fear can plant a deep mistrust among partners. Everyone has seen partners leave after a strategic reorientation or because of bad performance. A partner's performance is under permanent scrutiny. At the same time, a lawyer does not know if there will be work tomorrow. Every matter is finite, and the fear of an empty desk is pervasive.

The higher up the ladder you are, the more you have a say in matters concerning your law firm. Keeping that position in the wolf pack means you will occasionally have to bite inferior members

Partnership does not equal friendship. Even partners long in the game underestimate this fact. The relationships among colleague partners are remarkably different in law firms compared to in other workplaces. Real friendships are an exception. Partners tolerate each other, but having an office next to someone for 20 years does not necessarily result in loyalty. When a partner has left the firm, he or she will quickly learn that any contact stops. Former colleagues are simply not interested. At times, they cannot even bother answering your emails. Sometimes a firm succeeds in cultivating a body of alumni. This is purely out of an interest in personal gain on both sides and is not based on any remains of a collegial friendship. If this mistrust is ever confirmed in a spat between two lawyers, then the dislike they hold toward one another will be lifelong, and they will forever refuse to cooperate. Every firm will have at least one case like this.

Partners tolerate each other, but having an office next to someone for 20 years does not necessarily result in loyalty

Surprisingly, in the cases where partners move on to become in-house counsel, they do develop collegial bonds that can last throughout their entire careers. Not every lawyer in a law firm will be suited to work in-house, but the partners who make the switch behave differently when released from the clasp of the partnership. In a law firm, the lack of loyalty and fear of being ousted means there is a deep mistrust among partners.

The same distrust does not necessarily stretch to encompass partners of peer firms. I once knew a top litigation partner at a first-tier law firm. He was one of its most senior partners and had long been with the firm. Whenever he had work that he could not do himself, he would consistently refer it to a partner of the directly competing firm rather than give it to any of his colleague partners within his own firm. He was deeply convinced that nobody in his own firm could live up to his standards. Indeed, the insecurity coupled with the mistrust toward fellow partners will make every partner convinced that things are done much better at the competition: "At *that* firm, everything is professional and well organized!"

It is a seemingly bipolar behavior. On the one hand, nobody else is good enough, yet on the other, partners do not want it discovered that they themselves feel like a fraud. It is a characteristic that at times leads to manic-depressive manifestations. When work is flowing and matters are making headlines, a partner will dismiss everyone without politeness because they cannot be bothered with insignificant issues. Collegial spats or general running of the firm are for those without a successful practice to tend to. When work is ebbing and they have time on their hands, the looming hourly target presses upon them and they submerge themselves in insignificant details because that is what they do by default, and if they look very busy, then it is less likely others will notice that their performance is slipping.

This is especially applicable to practice areas that tend to have work in bursts or be cyclical, such as mergers and acquisitions and litigation. Predominantly advisory practices tend to have a more even flow.

This deeply rooted distrust is why client management has the propensity to be so difficult in law firms. Client management is about sharing knowledge about your client with other partners. Outsiders do not comprehend why centrally managing the knowledge about one client, for the common good of all, tends to be so difficult to implement in a law firm. The HR department may treat this issue as a function of a well-operating internal communication system. A suboptimal client management, where each partner works as an island, is the result of mechanical issues. A fancy intranet, encompassing blog functions and other high-tech aids, is installed. Sometimes an example of failing client management is even pinpointed as a culture question for the particular firm. Because law firm cultures traditionally have rewarded rainmakers, particularly when their contribution is isolated and does not generate cross-selling, internal communication about a client has not been encouraged. A fully collaborative culture tends to push heavy hitters away because they reasonably do not like to share more than they must with other partners. However, this tendency overlooks that the fundamental driver of trust that needs to be present among partners simply is not there. Lack of communication surrounding a client cannot be solved simply through the availability of a state-of-the-art intranet. When client management is functioning well, technical tools can aid in increasing efficiency. Instilling trust between partners is a gargantuan task that no HR team-building exercise in the world can achieve.

This deeply rooted distrust is why client management has the propensity to be so difficult in law firms

Lack of communication surrounding a client cannot be solved simply through the availability of a state-of-the-art intranet

Focus on detail, feeling of insecurity, and fear of being ousted: the behavior of partners boils down to these three drivers. Many seemingly incomprehensible decisions or actions will make sense when explained from these viewpoints. "Managing lawyers is like herding cats" is how the saying goes, but this is a simplistic catchphrase that is used in slapdash articles that base their success on human beings' yearning for easy explanations. Dissecting the personalities of lawyers may seem like idle talk with little bearing on any serious conclusions for the survival of law firms. This is where people are mistaken, though. The drivers that explain how partners will act in the running of their own firm are profound in their consequences and therefore paramount to understand. When it comes to running a business, all of these character traits will constitute a weakness. They stand in the way of a law firm forming a strategy and implementing it. In times when the market is monumentally shifting, such internal stumbling blocks in a law firm may be the firm's undoing. The internal disruptors are far more dangerous than any competition.

The drivers that explain how partners will act in the running of their own firm are profound in their consequences and therefore paramount to understand

Starting with the managing partner position, a law firm is peculiar in that it will elect one or two of its partners to govern the firm for a fixed period. This practice has several disadvantages. First, the partners are unlikely to have prior experience in strategically governing a business. This shortcoming could be overcome with good advisors, but the fact remains that no other business with a multimillion turnover would chose a CEO with absolutely no prior record. Second, they likely do not know how to move forward or what to do. How could they? Having a vision is normally something highly suspect for a lawyer. Tower Snow Jr. had vision. It did not end well. As explained, a lawyer is all about details. Taking a helicopter view and identifying the overall target is perhaps something talented lawyers can do in their own practice, but in leading a business, their view would be of terra incognita. Unfamiliar territory is not where a lawyer likes to operate. The third factor is the one leading to the most constraints. Managing partners need to get back into practice when their mandated period ends. They know their own practice is dwindling because they have no time to tend to it, as they are pulled into running the firm. At the back of their minds is that nagging fear that they may be made to leave a few years down the line as a result. Knowing they have to build up their practice again and being afraid of being ousted may prevent managing partners from making tough decisions. They cannot afford enemies. There is always a day of reckoning, and knowing it is coming influences the decisions they make, or refrain from making, even to the detriment of the firm.

Perhaps the most important consequence, flowing from the identified character traits of a lawyer, is the constant dynamics of the weakest. The bottom 20 percent of partners on the list ranking them according to performance will have a tremendous influence on the firm. The goal is to stay on for as long as possible—at all costs. Every extra year is worth a lot of money. Being ousted means that such a partner will have to move on to his or her own far less profitable practice and lose status in equal measure. Partners in the bottom 20 percent will keep a low profile. A partner is used to not having "friends," so the psychological pressure of being disliked is not overly hard to bear. Drawing attention to himself or herself is not wise, since the partner may become the next one to be made to leave. This leads to problematic behavior not so much in the decision-making process as when it comes to implementation. Due to the urge to keep a low profile, weak partners will vote in accordance with the strong partners or the majority even if it is a decision that is detrimental to themselves. Weak partners may even openly promote a strategic decision that, on a closer look, is damaging to their position or profit share, all to avoid being seen as obstructive or becoming a target for displeasure that may lead to them being ousted. However, once the decision has been voted through, this partner has no intention of executing it and might even sabotage it. Even if an important decision has been voted through with 100 percent of the votes, it does not mean it will be executed. On the contrary, it probably means it was so detrimental to the bottom 20 percent that nobody made a noise in opposition, and everyone is resolute not to aid its fruition. Here is a typical example that most law firms will have experienced.

Meet Peter. Peter is a 45-year-old partner with an intellectual property practice focused on copyright and trademark, which has gradually declined over the past five years. A discussion in the management team has led to the conclusion that it would be better if Peter could shift the focus of his practice to intellectual property and privacy. Some of Peter's peers have done so successfully, and this market is growing. Everyone, including Peter, agrees that this segment will be successful. And still nothing will happen.

Taking a look at Peter's practice one year down the line, it will still be the same and may have shrunk further. Why? Because the fear of letting go of current clients without knowing if you will have clients tomorrow is too paralyzing. The fear of an empty desk is central and urges every lawyer to accept almost any work. The fear of ending up in the lower parts of the 20 percent, and being ousted as a result, will prevent Peter from risking a position in the upper part of the bottom 20 percent. Having a small dwindling practice is better than having none at all. Nine out of 10 times, the very fact that the partner had this decision imposed on him or her will be used as the reason he or she gives for bad performance: "*You* said I had to change my practice, and now I do not meet my turnover target, and that's your fault!" This line will be used to stretch it out for a few more years. Management has to take great care in those types of strategy-forming discussions. Too much arm twisting will be used against the firm for years. Another often used excuse is the hourly target: "If I didn't have such a big hourly target to achieve, then I would have time over to cooperate more and publish more. But this target is imposed on me by you!" This way, the bottom 5 percent of the firm rules while having become the "backpacks" with the extra weight that the other partners have to carry for years. They are constantly busy playing political games with the goal of hanging on for another year, looking only for threats and not for opportunities. Sometimes, partners in the bottom 20 percent form symbiotic alliances with more successful partners. Rather than becoming a backpack, an otherwise poorly performing partner can play a central role in the practice of a better-earning partner in exchange for protection. The more successful partner, happy to have his or her turnover improved with proportionally little effort—thanks to the help of a lower-performing partner—may stave off an ousting of his or her helper and point the finger elsewhere.

An outsider will be forgiven for believing that any partner nomination is governed strictly by profitability. It is not

All strategic decisions, including creating a new partner, will fall victim to the same twisted mechanisms at work in a law firm. An outsider will be forgiven for believing that any partner nomination is governed strictly by profitability. It is not. Partners in a law firm with a shared profit pool should not take on a new partner who would not increase the value per point sufficiently for each individual partner to reap enough benefit. And yet they do.

Nominating a partner is a very delicate procedure born out of human needs, fraught with political considerations. Often, a practice group will have a senior associate who is particularly valuable to one of its partners. As mentioned earlier, a partner can build his or her practice around one or more senior associates and be relatively successful. When such a senior associate makes a request for a partner nomination, the partner who is asked is unlikely to say no. The other partners in the practice group may agree to support this nomination because getting a partner nominated means that the practice matters. It signals the strength of the practice within the firm. It is treated as proof that this practice is not being marginalized, which makes being the target of the next strategy realignment less likely. By making a partner nomination, the partners of that particular practice area are edged a bit further away from being ousted. The need to counter this fear is stronger than the possible dilution of the value per profit point. If the partner nomination does not go through, the practice group can use this failure as an excuse for years. The firm's lack of support and the fact that the practice has been denied the opportunity to invest in its future will be blamed for any disappointing revenues. However, the partner nomination may also go through. A number of partners in other practice groups may have their own candidates lined up, and if they do not vote in favor of this nomination, their own—much better—candidate's nomination a year down the line will be obstructed in retaliation. And so partners who, strictly speaking, do not meet partner criteria, are made. Little by little, the value per point ebbs away, and each strategic decision becomes even more difficult because the new partner is now part of the dynamic of the weakest and is trying to hang on for just another year.

At the other end of the spectrum, we have the top 20 percent of the partners. Here the problem is of a different kind, although it stems from the same drivers. Partners who are successful as lawyers tend to think they automatically know best when it comes to running the firm. Somehow, in everyone's minds, the success a partner has in being a lawyer is translated to mean that partner has an understanding of law firm strategy. The assumption is that the simple hierarchy of turnover will endow the ruling partners with an automatic leadership talent. If anyone in the top 20 percent explains how things are, they will not receive any criticism, especially not from the bottom 20 percent, for reasons explained previously. Partners outside of the top 20 percent tend to behave as well-paid employees, seemingly having no incentive to improve the business. Besides, because they keep their heads down to avoid any strong winds of discontent, the influence of the bottom 20 percent on the strategy of the law firm is so small that they feel they have no stake in running it. There is no responsibility taken for the direction of the firm. In fact, responsibility is denounced. It is easier to surrender to the self-proclaimed ruling capacities of the top 20 percent.

Somehow, in everyone's minds, the success a partner has in being a lawyer is translated to mean that partner has an understanding of law firm strategy

In their attempts to run the firm, many partners display another consequence of insecurity and attention to detail: the inability to prioritize. In areas outside a lawyer's area of competence, all details are equally important. If you are a person servicing airplanes, then attention to all details is a good thing. If you are a lawyer running your own business, the inability to separate issues that are important from those that are unimportant is a disability. Going berserk over a typo that has no bearing on the content of a report is not a proportionate reaction and is a result of a complete inability to prioritize.

This is not to say a typo is not bad—in a high-stakes business such as law, it comes across as evidence of poor quality and could potentially lead a client to think that there may be other overlooked mistakes—but the disproportionate attention and energy it receives is sometimes beyond all reason. Many members of supporting staff or junior fee earners can bear witness that such overreaction is common among lawyers.

Judging a flaw on its position in the great scheme of things requires an ability to see the big picture—an ability that many lawyers fall short of. Presented with a report on some aspect of the running of their firm, partners will immerse themselves in adjusting the text but not the content. In the meantime, management is swamped with complaints related to office equipment or how poor the flower arrangement looks in the reception area. Partners will write furious emails or make loud proclamations about matters that, to outsiders, seem trivial. When the iPhone was introduced, partners were furious their firm was still using BlackBerry. When the iPhone was adopted, the same partners were furious that it was difficult to type on them, yearning to get their BlackBerry's back. This behavior is often a way that partners mark their position, and it usually concerns an issue that involves an opinion rather than facts. Most partners will not risk losing face by receiving a counterargument from someone else who is better informed or smarter. An opinion cannot be used in this way. Making a complaint that will be taken seriously and dealt with marks a position. It also provides an excuse for why it is impossible to take action: "*How* can I be expected to take action on this client target list when the flowers in the reception area are atrocious and I am constantly hindered by the difficulty of typing on this iPhone?" The things that are blamed for any inabilities of a partner are always external. External reasons for failure must be found: the pitch was lost because it looked sloppy, a partner is not ranked in the client guide because the submission was appallingly written, and so on.

Management, made up of lawyers themselves, seldom sifts out the important complaints that have an impact on the running of the firm but instead tends to each complaint in turn with equal priority. The hours spent on meetings regarding the copy machines or the iPad covers often exceeds the amount of time spent on strategic issues. If a law firm is not vigilant to this slow process, little by little it will become a complaint culture that sickens the atmosphere and keeps management from doing the real work.

A friend told me a baffling story that perfectly illustrates this skewed approach to what is important and what is not. This friend is the head of IT in a large international law firm. In early 2014, we were talking about cybersecurity, and he described that his biggest concern at that moment was the news that had just broken regarding USB sticks carrying malware that can completely take over a PC, invisibly alter files installed from the memory stick, or even redirect the user's Internet traffic. The spyware can be implanted directly into the root of a computer, circumventing any virus scanner or firewall. He explained how these implants can, by design, even survive cleaning the hardware as well as software upgrades.

This is a serious risk for any law firm. Confidentiality is key. If a law firm is hacked and confidential client details are stolen, that is a very serious problem that could have consequences for the survival of the firm. My friend rightly considered it an urgent problem and had presented it to his firm's board. When we spoke again a few months later I asked about the measures taken to improve the cybersecurity only to find out that no actions had been taken at all. One of the measures my friend had proposed was to reduce the number of USB stations and permit only a limited number of special USB sticks provided by the IT department to be used in the firm.

This measure makes sense and is not expensive. However, from the lawyers' viewpoint, it was intrusive and restricted their manner of working. Cybersecurity is a very abstract problem for them. The risk is perceived as very low, and USB sticks are considered very handy by lawyers. They use them to take work between workstations, in the office, at home, and on vacation. In the same period as my friend was cautioning them about this cyber threat, some partners had loudly complained about their iPhones' protective covers. The quality was bad, and they had started to crack after just a few weeks of use.

My friend was summoned urgently to appear in a board meeting in which he was ordered to take action on the iPhone covers with priority. He had to provide everyone with new covers of better quality within a week. Nothing was said about the cybersecurity issue with potentially catastrophic consequences. This is a story that would baffle a CEO in any business. And yet, it is not an isolated case. It is emblematic for how a law firm is often managed. No matter how much new managing partners are burning with enthusiasm to get cracking with the big issues, they will find themselves bogged down in micromanagement within months.

This management behavior, exhibited by managing partners and other partners throughout a law firm, is very often a self-inhibiting process. Each staff member has as many bosses as there are partners. But the most crucial problem is that most partners—as well as many lawyers irrespective of age or rank—approach staff from one perspective: fee earner versus fee burner. No matter how many mixed office parties or fancy titles there are for staff members, it still comes down to this ancient divide. Staff who would normally play an advisory role in other types of businesses are instead asked for specific output in a law firm. This emphasizes the master–servant undercurrent. Combine this with lawyers' tendencies to manage details without prioritizing and you have a workplace most people with a high-value education will shun. This means that a law firm will have a hard time employing and keeping the level of professionals it needs for the future, such as project managers, information technologists, systems engineers, pricing professionals, as well as market and data analysts. Professionals at this level simply will not stand for the treatment they are likely to receive in a law firm and they will usually be offered better conditions in another type of business.

Staff who would play an advisory role in other types of businesses are instead asked for a specific output when working in a law firm

Lawyers' inner insecurity will also drive partners to make comparisons with peer firms, where everything is obviously better. At peer firms, staff members are sharper and more professional. If a peer firm has a new website, the website of the insecure partner's firm will be ransacked for faults. To be sure, there will be a few. If a peer firm has a new project, then panic will set a similar project in motion. This looking across the fence is very unproductive. Law firms should keep an eye on what the competition is doing, but it must be done with more self-confidence. The grass is not always greener on the other side. A law firm's way of constantly comparing itself to the eternally better competition is limiting and keeps it from looking for opportunities in the market instead.

Lawyers presuppose, when faced with making a choice, that there is such a thing as a rational decision. Rational decisions do not exist. Zero risk is a fiction. As the Danish physicist and Nobel Prize winner Niels Bohr cleverly put it: "Prediction is very difficult, especially if it is about the future." Every strategic decision is based on estimates of the future. Every prediction, by definition, comes with a degree of uncertainty. The very notion of uncertainty clashes with the character of a lawyer. The search for a perfect decision leads to endless contributions on harmless details. Lawyers are trained to dissect the arguments made, not to spot the arguments that were not made. If there is a proposal on the table, then its content will be examined in every detail, but nobody will look to see if any dimension is missing. Does this vision make sense? Could it lead to the desired outcome?

Evaluating the vision of a particular strategy, or the picture in which a decision fits, is not within the natural scope of what lawyers do. A lack of ability to see the potential consequences of a decision makes it hard for lawyers to take a stance. If an outcome is too uncertain, then no decision can really be made. This is another reason why plans are never executed. The enemy within not only is the obstructing behavior of the bottom 20 percent, or the counterproductive wailing over inconsequential details, it is also the love of theory over action.

There is an often cited cartoon from *The New Yorker* that cleverly depicts the preference for thinking about things rather than doing them. The cartoon shows a perplexed person standing before the choice of two doors. One door says HEAVEN. The other says BOOKS ABOUT HEAVEN. The fact that the person is hesitating when confronted with these choices is funny because we all know there is some truth to this absurd conundrum. We recognize that a lot of people may be tempted to read books about heaven rather than actually experience it. This especially applies to lawyers. If we just read up on it a bit more, do some extra research or hire that guru consultant, then alternatives on what we can do will become clearer. Let us read up on heaven before we go there. We tend to think that possibilities are always there—they just have not been unearthed yet. The preparatory phase will help law firm management to see all the possibilities and make an informed choice. What few understand is that not taking action is in itself very harmful.

What few understand is that not taking action is in itself very harmful

For a start, many possibilities actually come out of action. Taking action is what creates possibilities that did not exist before. We do not fully realize that we always look out at the future only from the spot at which we are standing. Simply getting to a different spot will open up new possibilities that were not an option before. Getting to a different spot necessitates taking action, starting with one partner at a time or practice area by practice area. But action entails risk. Clinging to abstraction helps us avoid taking action, and as long as we are not taking action, we will not be moving in the wrong direction. The risk of damage, in all of its forms, has been postponed and will soon be eliminated with a bit more preparation. Breaking this paralysis is important for all businesses. Recognizing this inertia, many companies focus on making continuous improvements in small ways instead of making radical, drastic changes to business infrastructure and processes.

The Japanese have a name for the method of getting better through small, continuous improvements: *kaizen*. When applied to the workplace, kaizen refers to activities that continually improve all functions and involve all employees. It is often applied to processes, such as purchasing and logistics, but also applies to management. A little-known fact is that kaizen was introduced to Japan by the United States after World War II as a way to help restart its economy. The method of small, continuous improvements was developed by Depression-era American business management theorists in order to build the arsenal that helped to win World War II. In 1940, the United States established the Training Within Industry Service (TWI) to increase production output to support war efforts of the Allied Forces. A manual created by the US government to help companies implement this business philosophy urged factory supervisors to "look for hundreds of small things you can improve. Don't try to plan a whole new department layout—or go after a big installation of new equipment. There isn't time for these major items. Look for improvements on existing jobs with your present equipment."[2]

After the defeat of Japan, the United States introduced the concept of small, continuous improvements to Japanese factories to help revitalize Japan's economy. A former TWI trainer and his group were contracted to go to Japan and set up a training process. The principles taught by TWI became a part of Japanese business management and became known to the world as kaizen. [3] For the sake of clarity: for a law firm, improving the copy machines, iPhone covers, or flower arrangements is not kaizen.

When having to operate in a field that is not within their expertise, such as the running of a business, lawyers tend to become paralyzed by the planning phase. No matter how much the plan is tweaked or shored up by research and statistics, the outcome will always look too uncertain to them. So they order a bit more research and get the opinions of more consultants in order to gain confidence. And so, the target list of clients remains just a list. "Let's make a better list before we take action!" This endless preparation phase is somehow not seen as inaction. Nobody considers the inability to decide to be a decision. Refusing to choose is not a choice. And yet, that is exactly what it is, camouflaged as thoroughness. This inability to move forward is an action in itself, only we do not appreciate the consequences because they are slow, chronic, and not obvious. That makes them worse. A practice, or an entire law firm, will edge itself little by little beyond the point of no return.

An outside force, in the shape of a guru consultant, MBA training, or a merger, must miraculously solve the problems of a partner, a practice, or the entire firm

This deadlock leads to an irrational but deeply rooted desire for deus ex machina solutions. An outside force, in the form of a guru consultant, MBA training, or a merger, must miraculously solve the problems of a partner, a practice, or the entire firm. An entire apparatus has grown up around this addiction, feeding off the insecurity of lawyers, providing them with endless training and courses that serve as nothing but excuses from taking real action. It is just as detrimental as the enemy within because it undermines a law firm's ability to take action for survival. The next chapter highlights the industry that has arisen around this false need and the damage it is causing.

KEY POINT

- All the characteristics that make a great partner turn into a massive hindrance when it comes to managing the firm.

9

HORSE WHISPERERS ARE DANGEROUS

Successful lawyers are often likened to sharks. A company, standing to lose much in a conflict, will want to hire a "shark" to look after its interests and achieve the best possible results. Given equal legal skills, a corporate client offered the choice between a well-rounded emphatic person in touch with his or her inner self or a thick-skinned predator obsessed with reaching the desired outcome will surely choose the latter, even if it is not a bet-the-farm case.

Personally, I prefer to liken lawyers to wolves rather than sharks. A wolf is an individualistic yet pack animal that is at its heart an untamable and patient hunter. And yet, a pack of wolves willingly surrounds itself with people who want to domesticate them.

I have explained how the inner drivers of partners in a law firm leave them vulnerable to a deeply rooted desire for deus ex machina solutions. In ancient Greek tragedy, a seemingly unsolvable problem was suddenly resolved by the contrived and unexpected intervention of a new character, ability, or object. An outside force must miraculously solve the problems of a partner, a practice, or the entire firm. This could be the guru consultant, personality testing programs, a merger with another firm, more training, along with numerous other promises of solutions. "We *need* this! It will solve everything!" There is

The yearning for salvation from the outside has such a strong pull not because it is a guide on how to take action, but because it is an alternative to taking action

always the next magic fix. What nobody seems to understand is that the yearning for salvation from the outside has such a strong pull not because it is a guide on how to take action but because it is an *alternative* to taking action. It is a way of postponing action while getting better prepared.

Only, lawyers will spend forever getting better prepared. In a case file, it is the deadlines of others—the client, the court, or the opponent—that forces work to get finished. A lawyer's insecurity and paralyzing fixation on flaws and threats needs constant feeding, and there is a hoard of people standing by to do it. An entire cottage industry has grown up around the notion of the lawyer as an unfinished HR project—a target for improvement. I call this the "soft sector" for lack of a better term.

The business of providing training and development opportunities to employees grew up around corporations in general and eventually spread to law firms. Employees should have opportunities to develop and to grow. Servicing employees with training has become synonymous with being a good employer. If providing a budget for training was ever treated as a way to increase stock performance and please shareholders, then this is no longer the case. The very notion of training seems to have changed from being a direct tool to improve employees' work-related skills to being the measure by which a company is judged to care—or not. The content on offer has come to increasingly focus on a person's inner life and personality as opposed to his or her work-related knowledge and skills.

It is important here to point out that there is a distinction between work-related skills training and behavioral training focusing on personality traits. There is training that is highly useful, such as skills training that conveys work-related facts or methods. For lawyers, this would mean a course in a legal subject. Compliance awareness or health and safety training are also examples of useful investments in human capital. My criticism is aimed at training that targets human behavior and psychology for the sake of changing the individual or group dynamics.

I am referring to the type of training or sessions that target the "stumbling blocks" that people carry with themselves, perhaps in the way they present themselves or how they communicate. Somehow, this type of training has evolved into an apparatus of different proportions from when it started. Personal development training was seen as fringe offerings in the mid-1970s. Today this kind of intervention is mainstream. Self-help gurus receive airtime on news programs, and company psychologists get to write their stories in the financial press. There is a management book focusing on behavior on every bestseller list. And in every village there is a provider of assertiveness training or someone who can teach you how to win an argument. Although it started as a supporting role, the soft sector has promoted itself to the position of moral backbone of a company.

This position comes from monopolizing the very definitions of what it is to be human. Arguing for adjustments in a company's "menu of care" has become tantamount to brandishing yourself as inhuman. It is as politically incorrect as being against diversity. Trying to expose the soft sector and its underlying armature of moralizing will have you brandished as cold and as mad as a hatter. And yet, I dare say the soft sector has been allowed to go to such lengths that even some employees start to feel that it is vaguely demeaning. Not willing to participate in a group session on how to improve communication with one another used to label you not a team player. These days, such withdrawal will brandish you as abnormal. Peer pressure, if nothing else, will get you into self-development.

Lawyers in particular will be misunderstood by nonlawyers. Often seen as cold, distant, and superior due to the nature of their profession, lawyers epitomize everything that self-helpers and self-improvers want to fix. And because lawyers do not particularly write or talk about themselves, a whole lot of other people have decided to do that for them. Historically, the divide between supportive staff and fee earners has been fraught with inequality and always led to a strained relationship. Having a monopoly on the definition of being human enables nonlawyers to have one up on a lawyer, not as revenge but as a tool for their own prosperity. Perhaps the soft sector has grown so popular because it is more raison d'être for the service providers than it is a need of the recipients. Another factor that drives the success of the soft sector is its perceived value. The activities that develop talent and potential, build human capital, and facilitate employability have been made into validations of worth. Self-actualization or personal development has come to be regarded as something occurring at the top of the organizational pyramid. Abraham Maslow's hierarchy of needs puts self-actualization at the top, defined as "the desire to become more and more what one is, to become everything that one is capable of becoming."[1] Recognition of the need for self-actualization has come to mean that firms invest in valuable employees. Through a twisted logic, the reasoning therefore goes: "Employees who are valuable receive investment; ergo, by demanding investment—and receiving it—I am a valuable employee." For many, not having courses or training in personal development on their CV is evidence of not being a prized professional with ambition. Its lack is perceived as reducing their employability.

Here is another strong and not entirely unimportant argument against behavioral-focused training for employees: *it does not work.* Human behavior is very complex. It takes years for a recovering alcoholic to control his or her addiction. Long periods of therapy by specialized professionals are required to address compulsive behavior or obsessions. How can we think that assertiveness training or a course on managerial behavior—"Speak with a deep voice and look people in the eye!"—will have any effect? Human behavior is not something for amateurs to play around with under the misguided impression that they will have an effect on it.

A robust character is central to being a good lawyer. If someone is in need of assertiveness training, life coaching, or personality testing, then he or she is better off in another profession

Personal development training may be slightly less harmful in most parts of corporate life. But for law firms, it is not only counterproductive, it is outright dangerous. A robust character is central to being a good lawyer. If someone is in need of assertiveness training, life coaching, or personality testing, then he or she is better off in another profession. If a lawyer encounters an aggressive counterpart, the immediate instinct should be to keep a cool head and respond in the way that is best for the case at hand. Sometimes that implies being aggressive, sometimes the opposite. If you first need training in how not to take things personally, then being a lawyer is not a good career choice for you. The same goes for work–life balance, as I touched upon in Chapter 6, "Ecce Homo." Work–life balance has become a central concept in business life. Gone are the days when people dedicated too much of their time to show an employer how much they valued their job—and rightly so. If an employer wants loyalty, he or she should buy a dog. But working hard hours as a lawyer is not being a slave to your employer or the hurdle you have to jump over to show you are more willing than others; it is simply what you have to do to become a good lawyer. To use sports as a metaphor, not every athlete has the right to partake in the Olympic Games. The ones who train hard and have talent are selected. Nobody would accept having to go with a team of inferior athletes simply because it is unduly harsh to ask them to train harder. People are not forced to become lawyers in law firms. If you want work–life balance, you should simply choose another career.

> *The gallery of forgotten management gurus is ever expanding, while the hype surrounding the current ones seems never to subside*

Personal development training, seminars, courses, and self-help books are abundant. Remember David H. Maister? He is a former Harvard Business School professor, American writer, and expert on the management of professional service firms. His theories were dragged into nearly every law firm board meeting a little over a decade ago in support of just about any argument. Was he right? To a great extent, yes. Did it help? It did not. The gallery of forgotten management gurus is ever expanding, while the hype surrounding the current ones never seems to subside. *Good to Great* by James C. Collins was quoted until it was coming out of our ears. The book looked at 11 companies that had made the leap from being good to becoming great and identified seven common characteristics. That information also did not change anything. Nine out of the 11 "great" companies used as examples in this bible among management books have survived. Most of those nine companies underperform on the S&P 500. They went from good to great to mediocre. Much the same can be said of the 1981 classic book *In Search of Excellence* by Tom Peters and Robert Waterman. No company success lasts forever.

My point is not that these books were wrong—which they were because of how they simplified things—my point is that management books are usually inconsequential. For a start, they always extrapolate from historical events: what have companies done that have made them successful? Historical actions will remain historical. They say nothing about the future strategy for other companies. And yet such books lead their readers to believe that the principles found among the high performers not only have made them good in the past but somehow form a universally applicable recipe for everyone in the future. Many management gurus operate by the method of first beating the world flat and then emphasizing one or several issues, which become the focus of all attention. They never seek out discomforting evidence. Stephen Covey, with his book *The Seven Habits of Highly Effective People*, is another example of compressing a complex topic into "easy" steps or schedules and figures. People love a magic bullet or an easy recipe, but they seldom go on to actually follow it. A management or self-help plan condensed to five easy steps may be satisfying for people to read, but it pointless for them to execute because it will not work. Then again, executing such a plan may not be the point.

When it comes to letting management gurus loose to theorize about law firms, they all start from the wrong premise or assumptions. Often, law firms are drawn up as caricatures, and the theory is built around that caricature. Rules that work for other businesses are applied to law firms in a one-size-fits-all approach and nearly always focus on marketing or acquisition of clients. Theories focusing on the individual lawyer, such as rainmaking, will mull over selling techniques, networking skills, or leveraging yourself. This all misses the essence of being a successful lawyer. The several really good lawyers I know have a few key traits in common, one of which is social skills. By this I do not mean that they are good at having a pleasant conversation with anyone or that they have a talent in maintaining a strong network. Instead, they all have the ability to read humans and know how to handle them to the benefit of the client. In the most crucial and pressing situations, they will be able to assess the dynamics and instantly adapt their behavior in the best interest of the case. A simple example: a partner I know is among the top when it comes to dispute resolution and is valued by clients because matters are usually resolved before they hit the courtroom. In a session with the opposing party, the discussion was edging closer to a subject that, if it ended up on the table, would be detrimental to the client. By immediately acting aggressively on one negotiation point, knowing that it would mean the forbidden topic would in bewilderment be forgotten, the matter was settled satisfactorily. Some would call it a knack for manipulation rather than social skills. I would say it is the ability to get people to where your client needs them to be. This ability is essential for a good lawyer, but it is something no management book or rainmaking manual in the world will teach.

The positive management books tend to come out of the United States, while the ones warning of danger—like this one—tend to come out of United Kingdom or the rest of Europe. Computers replacing lawyers, as predicted by Richard Susskind, worked for a while on the basis of stirring fear and the fact that lawyers are particularly uncomfortable with information technology. As pointed out previously, information technology is regularly used as the dead ringer for the traditional law firm. Automation and smart software is supposed to take over lawyers' work. Watson is still being treated as the looming shadow of future doom. Predictions of this kind play into lawyers' insecurities. Replacing all lawyers with a computer is nonsense. Computers will in the future probably replace the librarian and the trainee and even some young associates. They will eat into the commodity market. They are made for quantity, and today's programs can even deliver some quality. But an algorithm will not be able to replace all the qualities of a good lawyer—being worldly wise or creative, distinguishing fairness and reasonableness, possessing negotiation techniques or social skills. Above all, computers cannot innovate or be creative. Instead of being a disruptor, technology will offer the solution to the real threat: commoditization.

There is a wide spectrum of consultants that a law firm can hire. Many types of consultants are excellent champions of everything that keeps the soft sector going. They have for years helped law firms with finding their differentiators or coming up with a mission statement. As explained in Chapter 5, "Positioning," so-called differentiating factors belong to the code of the category and will not position your firm differently in relation to your peers. It is a red herring best ignored.

A mission statement was all the rage in the past decade, usually containing a phrase along the lines of "exceed expectations through our commitment to our clients, adding maximum value to their business." A mission statement is particularly useless because it is not only a hollow rallying cry but also a time waster. Many hours have been spent—and many consultants paid by the hour—by law firms formulating a mission statement. It goes on to spend a life in obscurity, hidden somewhere on a website or intranet, and taken out and dusted off when a journalist asks for it or a client request for proposal demands it. It has absolutely no consequences in reality.

A mission statement is particularly useless because it is not only a hollow rallying cry but also a time waster

Recently, Microsoft revamped its mission statement. It used to be "a computer at every desk and in every home." This statement is quite concrete, and the success factor is even measurable. The new mission statement goes: "At Microsoft, our mission is to enable people and businesses throughout the world to realized their full potential." Well, that clarified things.

Sarcasm aside, reading this mission statement hopefully makes it clear why no law firm should bother spending time revamping the mission statement they probably formulated a decade ago. The recent success of Microsoft has nothing to do with its mission statement but everything to do with the focus of its leadership. Let the mission statement lie and rest in peace.

Occasionally, consultants are hired because management has to go through the motions of having sought external advice even though the outcome has already been decided. The consultant's report is for the record. A report from a credible external source is needed to sell the decision internally among the other partners and legitimize what management has already decided to do. But irrespective of whether a consultant is hired as a mere ritual, and irrespective of whether the report produced has merit, almost all of them end up unimplemented in a drawer. A successful plan is about three things: implementation, implementation, and implementation. There is absolutely no substitute for taking action. Unfortunately, in many cases, the enemy within does not allow for this.

A person cannot take a course to fix a problem related to not taking action

Management gurus and their self-help books aside, there is an abundance of training, seminars, and courses on offer to lawyers. As pointed out earlier in this chapter, there are largely two types of training: training for acquiring or improving professional skills and training that focuses on the person, such as personal development or team building. The first type can be useful, such as a course on a legal topic for a lawyer. Other types of useful skills training can be account management, client management, presentation skills, and the like. However, although potentially useful, these last mentioned courses can all be found behind the door labeled BOOKS ABOUT HEAVEN. This is where lawyers enter who have been told to develop their practice and increase their turnover. Taking this kind of training enables them to tick the box that says, "I am doing something about it," while in fact stalling for time. I have witnessed dozens of training programs that lawyers have been sent on and known many of the lawyers coming out of them. Almost without exception, every partner attending has been enthusiastic. Never, ever has such training changed anything. Ever. Nobody went on to fix the problems in his or her shrinking practice. Everything remained just the same.

Training does not work. It is not because the participants are not smart or willing—they are. Nor is it because the people giving the training are not intent on passing on their knowledge to the best of their ability. It is simply because a person cannot take a course to fix a problem related to not taking action. An individual cannot experience heaven by reading about it. Skills training merely replaces taking action. It is the external salvation that participants hope will miraculously solve their practice problems. As I have said before, the best way to learn is to observe and copy someone who is better than yourself, and if you need boardroom advisors, your young lawyers must learn from boardroom advisors. The idea that instead of being sent on a course, a person should harshly be told that it is his or her own responsibility to start working on a real solution has never been allowed to flourish. It has long been suffocated in the manure of HR.

I once caught one marginalized practice group attending a course in cold calling. Not that there was any concern that anyone would actually go ahead and ruin any chances with potential clients by cold calling them because there would probably be a client list that needed improvement first. But the signal of desperation was cringe-worthy. They had run out of things to do (except for actually doing something). Cold calling is a marketing technique that is used to sell low-end products to unsophisticated buyers. Still, there is a surviving notion among lawyers that this is "selling" and is ultimately how to get new clients. This notion is born out of the deep desire for a quick fix. Likewise, an MBA will not be the solution to a lawyer's problem. MBAs fall into the same category as professional skills training. An MBA will not be the miraculous solution to the struggles a lawyer may have regarding his or her practice. It will only serve as a replacement for actually doing something.

Skills training may be harmful in the way that such interventions facilitate stalling for time by providing the illusion of added value while a law firm is slowly dying. The other types of courses, those that focus on the person, such as personality development or team building, are far more dangerous. The trends come and go. Personality testing instruments, such as the Myers-Briggs Type Indicator (MBTI) and the DISC Personality Test, were very popular recently. Some peddler is paid to put every person through a series of questions at the end of which participants are designated as either a color, a letter code, or a number. This is not only demeaning (although most test participants I have met did not object to being reduced to a digit), it is plain dangerous. The Myers-Briggs Foundation website states: "The purpose of the Myers-Briggs Type Indicator® (MBTI®) personality inventory is to make the theory of psychological types described by C. G. Jung understandable and useful in people's lives."[2] The MBTI was developed by mother and daughter Myers and Briggs, neither of whom had a formal psychological education, and is based on their knowledge of Jung. There is no scientific basis for this method. Apart from the fact that a company can just as well use the services of a Tarot card reader as use a personality indicator, this temptation of cataloguing people is harmful. Stereotyping people is one of the worst things you can do. Humans are complex. Looking at the best lawyers in the world, you will find they all have a very strong and multifaceted personality. Putting a label on someone is a sure way of killing off that person's potential and freedom to act. Nearly every law firm is now talking about "embedding creativity" while at the same time its lawyers are being reduced to a single label, color, or number.

There are more intricate forms of personal development training. I overheard a conversation in a law firm I visited where a nonlawyer was explaining to another member of staff that there were lawyers who had gone to see a horse whisperer. Horses are very sensitive animals, it was explained, and can pick up on the character traits of their handlers—even traits that the handler is unaware of. This person went on to paint a picture of how a horse can help with the process of understanding yourself. This may be true. Maybe horses do respond to the differences in people handling them, but sending a lawyer to see a horse, again, presupposes that there is a personality that needs fixing. The wisdom of improving people is never brought into question. It has now even led to professionals discuss horse whispering with a straight face at the coffee bar of a reputable business law firm. People's inner life has become fair game, and the ones who refuse to expose it are labeled cowards who are obviously afraid of self-analysis. This is absolute and utter tosh.

> *The wisdom of improving people is never brought into question*

Lucy Kellaway is the writer of a weekly column in the *Financial Times* and often describes the atrocities of corporate life in simple yet poignant and very droll columns. Subjects range from appraisals to imposed dress codes, from the myth that only humble leaders are successful to the uselessness of assessments. Every lawyer should read Kellaway's columns. In one post, she explains how a friend has to apply a new appraisal system with "mysterious attributes—such as 'leverages mastery' and 'innovates holistically.'"[3] Kellaway explains that this new system her friend must use applies to almost 100,000 employees worldwide and is found by all of their managers to be utterly idiotic. "But when I suggest it be scrapped she looks shocked. 'Out of the question,' she says. 'That would be interpreted as us saying we don't care about developing people.'"[4] Again, this is evidence of the HR monopoly on the definition of being human. Having to "develop" people has become gospel.

The *Washington Post* reported in 2015 that data from management research firm CEB shows that 6 percent of *Fortune* Global 500 companies have stopped using annual performance reviews and forced rankings.[5] Microsoft, Adobe, Gap, and Expedia are a few of the companies that have recently overhauled their employee review system. In 2015, both Accenture and Deloitte announced that they will stop using annual job appraisals for their own hundreds of thousands of employees. The reason they give, in a nutshell, is that annual appraisals do not work. "We are not sure that spending all that time in performance management has been yielding such a great outcome," said Accenture CEO Pierre Nanterme.[6]

This may sound strange, because both Accenture and Deloitte have for years been actively selling these types of appraisal systems to their clients. They now claim that these systems no longer fit the new I-want-it-now attitude of employees, where "instant performance management" is required. No doubt there will be a few consultancy hours charged to clients in the process of changing from the old system, but this is not where my criticism lies. Accenture and Deloitte are both consultancies, and they will go on and sell new ideas to any consenting adult who wants to buy them.

My criticism lies in the fact that there seem to have been so many companies that have thought these systems were a good idea, went on to buy them, and have spent years using them without any proven results. When the HR manager of a company comes knocking on the boardroom door, saying that implementing this annual performance appraisal system is a good idea, an intelligent management would surely say it sounds like nonsense, will be very expensive, and will not work. Apparently not. There is no employee who looks forward to the appraisal: to find out once a year if he or she has been doing a good job. No manager can really pinpoint the use of it but can easily testify to how much time and effort it consumes. They do it both because HR requires that piece of paper for its files and because the manager would otherwise be labeled as a bad manager and the employee as unmotivated or perhaps even hiding incompetence.

The recent conclusions that annual appraisals no longer fill a function is not, as Accenture and Deloitte will have it, a case of progressive insight. These systems were useless from the start. There was *never* an excuse to implement them. One would expect that law firms, of all businesses, would have taken a good look at what they were asked to implement and snubbed it because the argument in favor of such an annual appraisal system did not hold water. Instead, they went on and did what everyone else did.

In the fairytale "The Emperor's New Clothes" by Danish author Hans Christian Andersen, two fraudulent weavers promise an Emperor a new suit of clothes that is invisible to those who are unfit for their positions, stupid, or incompetent. The weavers' promise, against payment in gold, is a suit tailored from the most beautiful cloth that has ever been made. However, those who are stupid will not have the privilege of beholding the beautiful fabric. The Emperor accepts this proposition, as he is very vain. Since his subjects cater to his every whim, he is never contradicted and is not used to thinking for himself. However, the weavers do not weave and never intended to weave anything. They are frauds, out to profit from the vanity of the Emperor, cleverly protected by the human fear of being revealed as stupid. Nobody is going to expose the fraud for fear of being found incompetent. The clever weavers know that people are too conscious of being unmasked as ignorant to trust their own opinion. And indeed, when the Emperor parades for the first time in his new clothes, no one dares to say that they cannot see any clothes at all. In the tale, the deadlock is broken by a child who shouts that the Emperor is walking in his underwear.

Suddenly, everyone dares to acknowledge what they see and laugh. The Emperor hides in shame, and the two weavers are thrown in jail. In contrast to the people who think that the Emperor has no clothes on, but dare not say so, the systems of annual job appraisals do not have the excuse of having been implemented against better judgment. That would presuppose there was a judgment to start with. There was none.

Appraisals are merely the tip of an iceberg of similar drivel. Hopefully soon, big companies will have the epiphany that assessments, just as appraisals, do not work and that categorizing people according to a color or number is harmful. They may even realize that some MBA programs are useless. When that happens, I hope someone has the courage to say so. As long as everyone goes on mimicking each other for fear of being found stupid, nobody will shout that the Emperor is, in this case, stark naked.

Lawyers, who are usually critically minded, show no trace of critical thinking when agreeing to participate in increasingly fluffy training

It is incomprehensible that a majority choose to participate in this circus. Lawyers, who are usually critically minded, show no trace of critical thinking when agreeing to participate in increasingly fluffy training. Their usual skepticism to fly out the window when lapping up esoteric nonsense from a half-witted life coach. No Global Elite firm partners would let themselves be caught dead in a personal development session. It is not only killing for a partner's position; it is also something wholly undesired by an autonomous, self-reliant professional.

I was told at a firm about a session they had just had with one of their larger practice groups. They were all invited to sit in a room and told to discuss with the colleague sitting next to them improvements they felt should be made in their working environment. After a few minutes, the room was plunged into darkness, and the participants were told that lights had been installed under each chair. When a light under a chair lit up, that person was asked to share with the group what he or she had discussed with his or her colleague. The surprise element of darkness and lights under the chairs along with the group sharing was obviously an intricate ingredient of this session. Students may submit themselves to this kind of belittling treatment because they are aiming at the diploma at the end of it, but to have professionals undergo this kind of dubious group catharsis is potentially harmful.

Not so long ago, in the United States, there was a trend of visiting Native American sweat huts as means of team building, although luckily, it remained in the periphery of HR tastes and never became mainstream. As a team-building exercise, the group of colleagues would have to spend time naked in a sweat hut divulging personal secrets and desires, on occasion holding hands. Critically minded professionals who agree to take their clothes off to sweat together and subject themselves to serious tampering with their minds—it sounds too preposterous to be true. And yet it happened. I believe a tragic incident involving the deaths of some participants has subdued this fad, but it is nevertheless emblematic of how far this focus on the personal realm of individuals has been allowed to permeate business life as if it were a strategic part of it. It is not. It is detrimental to any strategy of a law firm.

No eyebrows are raised when we send lawyers on a team-building exercise that involves emotional prying

There is no point in teaching a boxer anything other than boxing. No serious professional boxing trainer would dream of it. And yet, no eyebrows are raised when we send lawyers on a team-building exercise that involves emotional prying. Buying into the soft sector is what allows two crying associates to get a partner told off for demanding higher-quality work. It breaks down the robustness and idiosyncrasies that make a good lawyer. It allows lawyers with underperforming practices to hang on for far longer than is good for the firm. Above all, it is demeaning. Leave people's personality and inner self alone. Allow everyone their own madness.

As much as I believe that we cannot change personalities, I do believe that we can change a law firm's culture. A culture is determined to a large extent by the theater in which it is staged and the roles people play on this stage. People act differently in different settings, like the child who changes schools and immediately starts behaving differently.

We have one role at our work and often a totally different role at home, and yet another one at our sports club or other recreational place. I know partners who were the gray mice of their firms, whom nobody attributed an ounce of backbone to, yet who left to open their own firms and transformed into bold decision makers leading successful and pioneering boutiques. There was no coaching involved or life changing experience. It was simply a role change and a different setting.

The culture of a law firm is like a blanket that covers its actors. Dynamics can be changed in order to achieve a different fabric in that blanket. In successful law firms, their culture is one of the determining factors in their success. Personal training will not change—or maintain—existing dynamics. Focus on teaching the individual new tricks will not bring about change in a law firm culture where all players remain in the same role. Nor will a focus on mechanical processes have any affect. Different procedures or high-tech tools to aid communication will not change anything. Sometimes, removing one or two people who have a big role in determining the undesirable culture is necessary.

Changing the environment also has an underestimated impact. People behave differently in a modern and more open building than they do in an old and conservative one. Everyone possesses a broad range of roles that they take on in order to adapt to the setting and the immediate people around them. There is no need to cajole enlightenment out of peoples' inner selves to achieve a change. It is also not a question of having someone perform a different job, requiring a different set of skills. It is not an HR solution involving shifting people around to different positions. Instead, change entails staging the theater differently to bring out other and more desirable roles. Breaking the routine of the previous play will change the sum of the individuals.

Without thought or scrutiny, horse whisperers have been allowed to influence the running of a law firm

Without thought or scrutiny, horse whisperers have been allowed to influence the running of a law firm. Lawyers themselves *are* the inner workings of a law firm. The legal business, more than most businesses, is based on people. Their attitudes, creativity, and brain power are what shapes a law firm. Surely, influencing and trying to shape those people would be an intricate part of carrying out a firm's strategy? And yet, few firms see the value of such an effort. The task is left to HR professionals because that is how it is done in every other business. Every business, surely, runs on a happy workforce? Courses, career development, and self-development are the only instruments to achieve a happy work force. Such offerings are all on the responsible employer's menu for its employees. This mold is hard to break. It will be a lonely job to go against this way of running a business. It certainly will not help you win a popularity contest. And yet, it is crucial for a law firm to take back this strategic tool into their own hands and place it higher up the boardroom agenda.

KEY POINTS

- Being completely absorbed by their profession and by their practice, partners have developed a strong craving for deus ex machina solutions when it comes to managing the business of their firm.
- This yearning for salvation from outside makes law firms vulnerable and easy prey for any guru, trainer, or consultant pretending to offer an easy solution.
- Following these false trails not only leads to postponing urgent action but also might dangerously weaken a firm to its core.

10

WHY PROFIT IS KEY

Dark clouds are forming heavily in the sky above the legal landscape, like huge wool packs heaping up in picturesque disorder, forming a menacing mass. The world may change only imperceptibly, little by little, but one day it is no longer the same. Many lawyers are so busy making their target, they do not look up to see their misfortune spelled on the horizon. Many business law firms will collapse in the next five years. There is no need to look into a crystal ball to be able to predict this.

Before summarizing the prediction of harder times ahead, it is fair to place the business model used by law firms so far into a wider perspective. Consulting has its Big Three, accounting its Big Four, and executive search its Big Five. But no corresponding clutch of dominant law firms has evolved. As pointed out in Chapter 2, "It's Not Like It Used to Be," the ten highest-grossing law firms together represent a mere 3.5 percent of the total legal industry turnover of $650 billion. Even so, the law firm business model has been one of the most successful business models of all. The return on investment for its owners has been tremendous. The longevity of law firms outperforms *Fortune* Global 500 companies. For as long as the list of failed top 100 law firms is in Chapter 1, "Icarus's Fall," and this list is by no means exhaustive, it may very well be that it is not as long as the list of failed *Fortune* 100 companies over the same time period. US magazine *Forbes* first came out with the now iconic *Forbes* top 100 companies in 1917. Out of those 100 companies, only one is still on the list: General Electric. In 1987, 18 of the original companies remained on the list. Some 61 had ceased to exist, and 21 had sunk in value. Since then, seven more have gone bankrupt or been acquired, and 10 more have sunk in relative value. The life span of *Fortune* Global 500 companies is continuing to decline. John Hagel and colleagues reported that the average life expectancy of a *Fortune* Global 500 company has declined from around 75 years in the 1950s to less than 15 years today, and it is still declining.[1] The longevity of business law firms has, until now, held up better. However, even for law firms, a successful business model yesterday does not mean it will be a successful business model tomorrow. Missing tectonic shifts in their markets was the undoing of many great *Fortune* Global 500 companies, such as Kodak, Motorola, and Nokia.

William Henderson of Indiana University has written about the macroeconomic perspective on the US legal market. The numbers show that law firms have had an incredibly good time for quite some decades. His work has shown that spending on legal services grew from 0.4 percent of America's GDP in 1978 to 1.8 percent in 2003.[2] The US legal business thus grew four times faster than the US economy. Further, legal services cost twice as much on average in 2011 as they did in 1985 in real terms. This level of growth cannot seem sustainable to anyone. Data from the Thomson Reuters Peer Monitor 2016[3] shows that the total billable hours recorded by firms did not grow in 2015. In fact, the overall pattern of the past five years shows the same stagnation. In other words, the demand for traditional law firm services has not increased.

The decade leading up to the economic collapse in 2008 was a time of unprecedented growth for law firms. On the whole, law firm partners during this period saw their firms' revenues and profits increase dramatically. This boom period came to a screeching halt in 2008, but by early 2010, the market began to improve and ultimately reached its current level of positive annual gains. Many firms in *American Lawyer*'s top 100, lacking the pricing power of the Global Elite or New York elite firms, maintained profits by cutting the number of people, including shedding equity partners. The 2008 crisis triggered an optimization overhaul in law firms. Underperformers were made to leave.

Shared services staff members were cut, and other overhead costs were scrutinized and cut where possible. Payments on outstanding invoices were chased, and the collection process was made more efficient. In many law firms, the lemon was squeezed hard and good. Much fat was cut away to make a leaner machine. Profit per equity partner (PEP) was kept level due to traditional optimization that increased profit. For many law firms, squeezing the lemon hid the real state of things. We are now reaching a point where, for many law firms, the lemon has no more juice in it. For the first time, we are about to enter the post–squeezed lemon era. Law firms will have to find other ways to increase profit in order to preserve the PEP. The old tricks will no longer work. This increase must come from elevated revenues generated in other ways than by cranking up the hourly rate. For that, law firms have to change their business model.

> *For the first time, we are about to enter the post–squeeze lemon era. Law firms will have to find other ways to increase profit in order to preserve the PEP*

Impending lawyer retirements, a massive intergenerational transfer of wealth that will take place over the coming decades, continued population growth, and the growing complexity of law and legal regulation have all been cited as the reasons that the legal market will grow and that law students can look forward to good job market conditions.[4] Even if this turns out to be true, it does not mean that it will benefit the business law firms of today. There is no denying that prices are going down and will continue to do so until the market correction is completed. A possible shortage of lawyers will not change this fact.

The global legal landscape has changed significantly in the past decade. Competition has increased tremendously. We have seen the emergence of the global law firm competing in several jurisdictions by servicing international clients and winning an increasing share of the panel package deals. From a client's perspective, these law firms are interchangeable, and although it might look like they are onto a winning strategy, most of them are struggling with profitability, or will be once the lemon is entirely squeezed. As clients expand globally, cross-border matters are becoming more the norm than the exception. For many law firms, this trend entails an increasing share of work coming through referrals, making their partners work as associates under the lead of a partner somewhere else. The Global Elite has come to virtually monopolize all the international bet-the-farm deals. At the same time, we are witnessing the formidable rise of the in-house lawyer. An increasing share of companies' legal work is now done in-house by smarter and better organized professionals who patrol their company's running operations, as well as through new initiatives, with the guidance of risk appetite. There is downward pressure on the price of legal services in all segments except the very top one. This price pressure will continue. Boutique law firms, created through partner groups that have broken away from larger, higher-end law firms, are offering high-quality advice at much lower prices. Alternative service providers have entered the market, lured by the higher profits of the last few decades. All these new entrants offer some combination of cheaper, faster, and better. Although computers will never replace lawyers, automation will eat into junior associates' hours, as low-skilled work can easily be performed by software. The entrance of technology will have other consequences for law firms than just letting go of some commoditized work. New service providers are often interdisciplinary, effortlessly integrating technology, process, and data into their services, something that law firms struggle to do. The lawyers who need to fight their way onto the legal market and into law firms must have more skills than what automation can replace. Creativity has already become key to the higher segments of legal practice. However, the single-most influential force on the legal market is the commoditization of law. Most legal work has become so common in clients' view that it must come at a lower price. More law firms are simply offering the same level of expertise. More of the same means commodity that comes with a lower price tag. As the commoditized segment increases, the bespoke segment is shrinking. Profitability is at serious risk under the traditional business model.

Most legal work has become so common in clients' view that it must come at a lower price

As changes converge to put pressure on the middle segment of the legal market, law firms look for ways to compete. We have seen law firms respond by expanding internationally either by satellite offices, mergers, or development of best friends. Some law firms believe that growth in the number of lawyers is required for their firms' continued success. As the 2014 Report on the State of the Legal Market formulates it, "Law firm leaders feel constrained to articulate some kind of strategic vision to help their firms weather the current storm, and the message that we need to 'build a bigger boat' is more politically palatable than a message that we need to fundamentally change the way we do our work."[5] Law firms are trying to keep up, ushering in pricing directors and project management. Some are outsourcing services that can be done cheaper elsewhere and coming up with new, flexible ways of working using pools of professionals on standby. And yet, hiding behind the news of the spectacular moves of players in the market, the majority of law firms are not doing much at all. The business model stays the same.

Perhaps it is the situation of the anecdote describing a frog slowly being boiled alive. The premise is that if a frog is placed in cold water that is then slowly heated, it will not perceive the danger and will be cooked to death. Profit has, more or less, always been part of the successful business model of law firms, to the extent that its vital importance is not evident—a case of "you don't know what you have until it is gone."

An article in the *Harvard Business Review* describes it in a very simple way: "The [professionals] we spoke with who rejected the notion of disruption in their industry cited the difficulty of getting large partnerships to agree on revolutionary strategies. They pointed to the purported impermeability of their brands and reputations. They claimed that too many things could never be commoditized in consulting [or law]. Why try something new, they asked, when what they've been doing has worked so well for so long?"[6] The 2015 Report on the State of the legal Market suggests the same dilemma as one of the root causes of law firms' inaction: "Given the restructuring that many firms have undertaken since 2008, the equity partners in the largest 200 US firms have fared reasonably well, even in the present market environment.

In 2013, profits per equity partner in these firms averaged $1.19m, not back to levels seen in 2007 but hardly disastrous. It is not surprising, therefore, that law firm leaders might have a difficult challenge in convincing their partners of the need to make fundamental changes in their business model or practices. As one observer of the legal market has quipped, 'It's hard to convince a room full of millionaires that what they're doing is wrong.'"[7] Law firms have been doing so well for so long that it is natural to think that good old days will return, and like all recessions, this one will eventually end. Why would Chicken Little be right this time? Or another quote, attributed to various people but used by Stephen Covey, whom I so ungraciously dismissed in Chapter 9, commenting on the fall of Detroit car manufacturers: "Nothing fails like success."

Law firms have been doing so well for so long that it is natural to think that good old days will return, and like all recessions, this one will eventually end. Why would Chicken Little be right this time?

Partner mobility will work as a catalyst in the downfall of business law firms. Nobody is disputing that there is an increased lateral movement of partners. Nearly every week there is an update on lateral moves between competing firms from one of the legal business media sources. Partners have reasons to either seek higher profits or transfer their practices from one firm to another, and law firms need a quick way to grow. In London, we have in the past years witnessed a war for talent between US and Magic Circle firms, which has sent the latter frantically reviewing their lockstep system. Studies have shown that once partners start moving, the tendency to move again is likely. They have in a sense become mercenaries, fighting on behalf of whoever pays the most or provides the most prestigious work. Usually, both go hand in hand. The old Cravath partnership model is failing for law firms other than Cravath. Partners are more occupied with themselves than with the firm. There are potential ways to build loyalty into a law firm's compensation model or contractually limit the ability to leave the firm by so-called departure lounge clauses or partner lock-ins. Some law firms have been reported in 2016 to be reviewing their partnership deeds in order to restrict the number of partners able to resign in any fiscal year, presumably in fear of drainage of partners while carrying out reforms or merger talks. Lock-in, an agreement with an individual partner that he or she will be financially punished if he or she leaves in a certain period, is usually used in preparation for a merger or reorganizations.

Looking a bit closer at why partners move, three motives emerge. The first motive is "forced" on partners who are made to leave because they do not make their targets or because they do not fit a realignment of the firm's strategy. These partners go on to form niche firms that offer decent-quality services at relatively low prices, or they join a firm in a segment slightly below the one they came from. The second motive is attributed to individuals or groups of partners whose practice areas are not supported sufficiently within their firms. Having a high-level practice in your field but being made to operate at the fringes of your firm is less and less accepted by partners as the market is breaking up to provide more opportunity for smaller, specialized firms. In the beginning, this scenario was often seen with intellectual property practices; however, today, even M&A practices break loose to form niche firms. The third motive is at work in individual partners who leave for a firm that they feel better reflects their level.

Law firms are at a crossroads. Twenty years ago, partners did not jump from one firm to another. Law firms were true partnerships kept in shape by the rigid scaffolding of a more or less egalitarian lockstep system. Being a lawyer meant exercising a profession very much like a doctor. You do not work as a lawyer—you *are* a lawyer. But law firms are increasingly forced to operate as businesses, guarding their profits, competing for talent, and striving for growth. At some point, the law firm as a company became more important than the profession itself. This change has gradually come upon us, but it seems to have been sprung upon many law firms. As a result, they find themselves struggling to adjust. Partners operating in a world of law as a profession will be left behind by the legal market, clinging to their status as profitability dwindles.

Merging the old viewpoint of being a profession with the new reality of having to be a business brings law firms into dangerous territory. They seem to be treating the balancing act between the two as a business model in itself: doing what they always did only a bit more efficiently or with new tools and methods. Instead, it is simply the permanent state of not making a choice, causing a firm to sink slowly into a segment that it cannot pull itself out of. The only answer is to completely surrender to being a business. It can be likened to professional soccer clubs: they are not about sport; they are about soccer as a business. Professional soccer clubs are honed businesses that operate to ensure the best players, formulate winning strategies, and acquire the best coaches. All of these factors are part of playing at the top of the game.

The business of a law firm must be built around profit. It is ultimately the only goal that matters in the law firm as a business and must be the guiding factor in all decisions. There is a difference here between, on the one hand, what the individual partners find to be a decent income at the end of the year and, on the other hand, profit as a business measure. To an individual, $800,000 might be just as fine as $900,000. It is all a lot and enough. But this misses the whole point of profit as a gauge that must be kept level or must increase in order to ensure continuation of the business.

As numerous examples show in Chapter 1, even a relatively slight decrease in profit can trigger a run on the bank and ensuing collapse. Profit must be kept on par with peers in the same segment; otherwise, the 10 best partners may leave. Partners often do not fathom the catastrophic impact their leaving would have on their firm. With few exceptions, the top 10 percent of a law firm's partners generate three times as much turnover as the bottom 10 percent. As demonstrated in Chapter 7, "The Financial Model," a relatively small decrease in a law firm's turnover translates into a much higher decrease in the profit because nearly all costs are fixed. This can be demonstrated again with a simple calculation. Say that we have a law firm with 100 partners generating a turnover of 2000. The top 10 partners generate 300 of the turnover, and the bottom 10 generates 100. The other 80 partners each generate the average, resulting in 1,600 together. We can count on using a fixed cost that roughly represents 65 percent of the turnover, as is the case for many law firms. In this example, the costs would be 1,300 out of the 2,000, leaving us with 700 in profit. If the top 10 partners leave, this will decimate the turnover by 300, or by 15 percent. But the cost remains 1,300, which means that the 300 comes straight off the profit, reducing it by 42 percent. What was a profit of 700 is, with the swipe of only 10 partners, reduced to 400. Few law firms will survive a 42 percent drop in profit. The second-best partners will immediately take action to leave for other firms, taking the best deal they can get. Nobody wants to be the last man standing. This is why profit is key. It is the gauge of a law firm's business and the measure that successful partners to go by.

A bit of a dip in profit may not matter much, but once the three-year average is down, the very top partners may start to look around if they have not already been contacted by headhunters

A lawyer will be measured, by himself or herself as well as by other lawyers, by two things: the type of matters he or she handles and the compensation he or she receives for it. A bit of a dip in profit may not matter much, but once the three-year average is down, the very top partners may start to look around if they have not already been contacted by headhunters. Every law firm has to ask itself: at what point will my best partners be snatched away? If those partners are compensated for a decline in profit, by getting to do the cutting edge of their practice in a team that is known in the market, they will be less inclined to leave. In general, above-average talented lawyers are more attracted to nicer work than nicer profits. The gifted lawyer wants to work with the other best lawyers in the market and will always seek the top end of clients and matters. This is the highest form of recognition. Any moderate fall in profit will not lure them away. But if their peers are equally praised elsewhere and their fellow partners are not the very best in their legal field, then the dip in compensation is enough to send them looking. This delicate equilibrium of reputation and compensation is the most sensitive at the very highest end of the market, while toward the middle and lower segments, the more commoditized work will make it matter less. It could very well be the case that the disparity between a law firm's best partners and the rest of the partners is so great that it is a rift that cannot be bridged. Law firms end up being held hostage by their top 10 partners. Keeping your best partners may not be the best thing to do. A split up and a clear strategy going for another profitable segment may be the best path to take.

The very large IBLs are less enslaved to maintaining this equilibrium. The most cutting-edge legal work is done by the firms with the highest PEP or top equity. The IBLs may be on the top of the list for global turnover but not when it comes to the PEP. A comparison of the number of lawyers in AmLaw 200 firms and the profits per partner of such firms shows that there is low correlation between firm size and profitability. But since the international business law firms are so large in headcount and do not always deal at the very top level (where partners are less replaceable), it does not matter if a few partners leave here and there. They have insulated themselves with a bit of fat. But a law firm whose very top partners attract the work for the whole firm, losing one partner may be repairable, but that one partner may just trigger the next one to also look around, and once two top partners go, the others will follow. In recent times, as reported by *The American Lawyer*, there is a growing interest among larger law firms to sell their uncollected billings to banks or investors. Like in factoring, the law firm receives cash in return for a cut of the outstanding amount. This shows an increasing need for law firms to prop up cash flow at the end of the year in order to pay partners and to boost revenue. These days, few firms can afford to end the year badly because their structure is fragile.

Understanding profitability is also key to the relationship with clients. The new legal marketplace is a buyer's market where clients increasingly dictate the pricing. A law firm that still thinks in terms of hours and turnover will not be able to survive value-based pricing, as outlined in Chapter 4, "What Goes Up." Under pressure from an increased number of alternative fee arrangements, the law firm that is focused on profit will reap the benefits.

To the outside world, law firms operate as businesses, making the adjustments that they have to in order to adapt to the market. And yet, at the most crucial moments, in nearly every law firm, there is a complete denial of this new world order. If a law firm was run as a business, partners would be created only on the basis of strategy and profit. They are not. If law firms were run as businesses, they would have a complete overview of the cost of every type of service and the margins they can operate with. They are far from it. They would have a sober view as to what they really are and what can realistically be achieved. Instead, a vast majority consider themselves a leader in corporate and mergers and acquisitions, the holy grail among practices. This inability to leave the old realm of law as a profession and make themselves business ready is constantly thwarted by the enemy within, as described in Chapter 8. The constant dynamics of the weakest and their desperate determination to hang on for another year festers within many law firms and stands in the way of a focus on profit. The management system prevents managing partners from making harsh decisions, if they succeed in prioritizing them in the first place. Unproductive comparisons with peer firms by self-doubting partners keep people away from the real work. The search for a perfect strategy leads to endless discussions of inconsequential details. A lack of focus has allowed the HR apparatus to undermine a law firm's ability to take action for survival by feeding its deeply rooted desire for deus ex machina solutions with red herrings. The core abilities of a good lawyer—a robust personality with an inner lust to argue and fight—are overlooked, and the plot is lost in the sea of psychobabble. At the same time, the inability to trust hired professionals to handle everything that lawyers should not handle themselves creates a counterproductive band of servants who merely carry out the bids of the sudden expertise of the top 20 percent partners. These are the reasons that law firms are not run as businesses.

The constant dynamics of the weakest and their desperate determination to hang on for another year festers within many law firms and stands in the way of a focus on profit

It must be emphasized that not every firm can strive for the profit margins of Wachtell Lipton or Quinn Emanuel. The Manhattanization of the legal business is a dangerous thing. For a law firm to strive toward a goal outside its segment is unrealistic and futile. Not every firm can or should be a Global Elite firm. A law firm must look only at itself in order to formulate a viable strategy—it cannot be done by copying another firm's business model. The simple question, *How can we ensure continuation and be as profitable as we possibly can be in our segment?*, must be guiding. Just like a professional baseball or football club, a firm must retain the most successful players that it can attract. This quest, though, is limited to a firm's own segment. Partners are acquired by market value, but it only matters what the going rate is within the given segment. Just as players are confined to their league in sports, a law firm's partners will not readily move to a higher segment. Partners in a law firm will remain with a firm only on the basis of implementing a strategy that at least maintains their current profit level and keeps them on par with peers.

Formulating a satisfying strategy is preceded by a realistic analysis of the firm itself. As pointed out, the syndrome of leading in corporate and mergers and acquisitions shows that wishful thinking is thriving. It seems law firms cannot withstand the lure of high-end work. In Greek mythology, the Sirens were beautiful but dangerous creatures who lured sailors with their enchanting voices to shipwreck against treacherous rocks. M&A and capital markets are the Sirens that bring law firms into dangerous waters. By aspiring to be the best in M&A or capital markets, a law firm pushes itself out into an arena where it may not be able to compete. The disconnection between ability and aspiration becomes misleading. Looking high above its place, such a firm will oust practices that do not measure up and cut away the areas in which it *can* compete. Being realistic is crucial to deciding what path to take. Starting off on the wrong premise will lead to the wrong destination.

The good news is that we are not in a shrinking market and that profitability can be reached by many distinct roads. Alas, for most firms, only one road at a time can be traveled. Even in the lower segments of law practice, there is much money to be made. It just requires a different business model. Often, law firms are sidetracked into believing it is a question of improving or changing its products: better, sharper, faster. This is not the case. It is their business model that needs an overhaul, and this is a totally different matter. A law firm aiming to operate profitably in the lower midmarket segment must by definition have low costs and make more hours. If you have two different business models, one with a blended rate of 400 and one with a blended rate of 200, and both want to reach the profit of 1000, then the one with a blended rate of 200 will need to make more hours and/or have much lower fixed costs. A child's arithmetic. This means that such a law firm must be equipped totally differently in comparison to a law firm that handles bespoke work: a cheaper location, increased automation, smart solutions for standardization, and high volume. This McLaw segment can be just as profitable as the three-star Michelin segment or other segments in between, but they can rarely be combined. A fast food restaurant would not attempt to serve food deserving of three Michelin stars under the same roof and make a profit. This is not only because it leads to difficulties in branding (how do you make the two concepts credible next to each other?) but also because the concepts are two totally different businesses. They do not operate in the same way on any level, be it purchasing, preparation, or sales. There would be no synergies to gain from. In the same manner, a law firm must be clear and realistic about its segment in order to be both profitable and sustainable in the long term. Mixing high-end and low-end work creates neither a credible offering nor a sustainable business model.

This McLaw segment can be just as profitable as the three-star Michelin segment or other segments in between, but they can rarely be combined

Having said this, there are examples of top-tier law firms responding to commoditization in a textbook perfect way. Allen & Overy has previously attempted to launch services that capture clients' low-value volume work by offering generic, low-cost, and accessible advice online. In 2015, the firm rebranded its efforts and launched Aosphere, a site that offers a wide range of services, including G20 reporting requirements, derivatives clearing, shareholding disclosure, marketing restrictions, and cross-border data transfer. These services are particularly welcome to the firm's large financial clients. The lower price point is not damaging to the Allen & Overy brand because of the innovative use of automation and software, which makes it a separate but high-quality offering that will not devalue partners' bespoke advice. Not long after launching Aosphere, Allen & Overy revealed MarginMatrix, a technology-driven service that helps banks handle incoming global regulation of the $500 trillion over-the-counter (OTC) derivatives market. Reviewing all contracts for compliance and creating new documents is a massive job. According to Allen & Overy's own estimate, the 10,000 OTC contracts a major bank would normally hold would take 15 years of lawyer hours to process, while MarginMatrix will be able to do it in 12 weeks with only one person deploying the system. But the added stroke of genius is that the handling of the system will be done by Deloitte with which Allen & Overy has teamed up with for this specific purpose. Since there will still be a lot of work around execution of the contracts that MarginMatrix provides, a party will be needed that is good at handling large projects at a predictable cost. Deloitte will be able to provide project management to large teams of negotiators in multiple jurisdictions in a way that Allen & Overy will not be able to do. What these two examples show perfectly is the response to commoditization by using technology.

Another example of commoditization and responses thereto is the airline industry. As little as two decades ago, the traditional airlines, usually the pride of their respective country, were still firmly planted in the world of air travel as we knew it. In the United States, the 1978 Airline Deregulation Act partially shifted control over air travel from the political to the market sphere. Further, the CAB Sunset Act phased out the control of the Civil Aeronautics Board (CAB), which had, up until its closure in 1984, controlled the airline market almost completely. Low-cost carriers proceeded to challenge the legacy airlines, including American, United, Continental, Northwest, and Delta, that were the champions before deregulation. Later in Europe, the 1992 deregulation of the air industry created a larger market for airlines and presented an opportunity for local low-cost carriers to expand. Among the first ones were Ryanair and EasyJet. The coming of the Internet enabled online booking, which cut flight prices even further by selling directly to passengers and excluding the costs imposed by travel agents. The initial reaction of the incumbents was to do nothing. They simply did not believe that it was *their* passengers that the low-cost carriers would service. They underestimated the effects of the commoditization of airline travel.

As history now shows, a large part of midmarket segment of travelers turned out to want to fly from A to B as cheaply as possible. Service levels, inclusive on-board meals, connecting flights, or even landing at a hub airport all turned out be less important than a low price.

After having seen dropping passenger levels and waning profits, the incumbent airlines started to open up their own low-cost branches to compete. However, the new entrants did not, and still do not, compete on the same terms as the legacy carriers: they have entirely different organizational models. Trying to combine the two business models has proven cumbersome. Air France-KLM has been hit by pilot strikes when trying to manage its high-end and low-cost (Transavia) branches differently. German airline Lufthansa has also been hard hit by pilot strikes for the same reasons. Operations, cost management, pricing, and sales are all completely different when comparing high-end and low-cost airlines, because they operate in different segments of the market. Still, they have the same profit goal. There are airlines that have honed in on the high-end segment of the market. Emirates launched a San Francisco–Dubai route in August 2015 with first-class suite return tickets at $30,000. This is not even the most high-end ticket on sale. First class is booming just as much as the no-frills segment. Emirates and other airlines like it have positioned themselves as providers of high-end air travel. Whether a company chooses high-end or no-frills business models, when carried out properly, they can both lead to the same profit and longevity. This example of the low-cost carrier disruptors in the airline market serves a useful analogy for where law firms find themselves today. If they can only resist the Sirens.

The most changes in the legal market that have yet to occur will take place in the midsegment. This is where 90 percent of all business law firms are. This is also the segment where law firms are the most vulnerable. This is where law firms are least likely to make a clear choice of strategy. This is where most law firms, failing to recognize their true market position, insist on aspiring to be one of the top firms, way above their segment. In the midsegment, competition is the strongest and commoditization is expanding, putting pressure on the profit model.

In short, then, two stumbling blocks to the survival of many law firms have been identified: the failure to recognize the key role of profit and the inability to choose a realistic business formula in an increasingly commoditized market. All of this might seem obvious. And yet it happens for all the reasons just explained. This is not unavoidable or irreversible. Many law firms can avoid succumbing to either slow decline or sudden death—if they take action. It would be unfair to say it is a predicament that they can solve alone. Baron Munchhausen succeeded in rescuing himself from drowning by pulling on his own hair. But he also rode a cannonball, traveled to the Moon, and mended his horse with laurel tree branches when the animal was accidentally cut in two. Law firms are not capable of such impossible feats. They need help from more than fairytales.

The bad news is that the way out is not easy. There is no quick fix in 10 easy steps. There are no shortcuts. It starts by looking in the mirror, which in itself is usually done with great reluctance. A realistic self-image can be achieved only by a ruthless analysis. This is essential, as otherwise, there is no chance of formulating a realistic strategy, and the project will fail miserably.

The next step, formulating a strategy, is also not an easy task. There is no one-size-fits all recipe, and it does not help to peek at the neighbors. Copying simply does not work. There is a solution for each law firm, and every one involves change. But if you could read about the detailed answer on how to thrive in a commoditized market in this book, then I would have provided the deus ex machina solution that I preach does not exist. The particular strengths and weaknesses of a firm are unique, and it has to operate in a market with a unique constellation of features. Identifying the opportunities in the market and envisioning the opportunities of tomorrow takes vision. Even then, a law firm is not safe. Next comes implementation. As illustrated, all partners may vote yes on a strategy, but there will be little intention to implement anything new at all. Crucial throughout such a process is to manage the partner group. The process of restructuring must not itself become the lit fuse in the barrel of gunpowder. Headhunters may be standing at the gates, ready to swoop in on the best partners. Implementation also takes persistence. Even the best of plans have fallen by the wayside. The shackles of the profession of being a lawyer pose a formidable hurdle for the transformation of a law firm

The shackles of the profession of being a lawyer pose a formidable hurdle for the transformation of a law firm. The enemy within is the more difficult one to fight

into a pure business. The enemy within is the more difficult one to fight. Execution of the chosen strategy has to be relentless.

These are many ifs—perhaps too many. "The death of a law firm" may sound overdramatized, but the prediction is nonetheless likely and the results nonetheless frightening. It is heartening, then, that lawyers, supported by a robust personality and driven by a fighting spirit, will not go gently into the good night. The weak hearted will wither and moan. Only the strong will continue.

FINAL THOUGHTS

Being successful is a dangerous thing—even more so if the success has lasted for a long period of time. Over the past decades, business law firms have been extremely successful. Partner profit shares have risen more than anyone could have imagined 25 years ago.

Doom has been predicted for the legal profession multiple times before. IT would make lawyers obsolete. IT did not. Clients would refuse to pay the increasingly high hourly rates. They did not. The 2008 financial crisis slashed the finance and M&A markets. They have since bounced back to higher levels than before. With all these examples, and there are many more, partners will be forgiven for thinking that the business of selling legal services is invulnerable and immune to disruption in the long term.

However, this attitude might prove to be a costly mistake. Although none of the trends so far have led to the end of lawyers or even to a permanent disruption, they are slowly, surely, and irreversibly eating their way into the profitability of business law, thus undermining the very foundation that made this profession so successful in the first place.

The board of Kodak at one point aborted the further development of digital photography (even though it was one of the pioneers and market leaders in this field) because it would cannibalize Kodak's highly profitable light-sensitive film operations. As we all know, it turned out to be a fatal error of judgment.

Today, the legal industry stands at a historical crossroads, facing equally fundamental decisions. While the traditional business model for most law firms may have reached the end of its life cycle, there are multiple equally profitable alternatives. Getting to them requires a brutally honest look in the mirror and a rigorous self-analysis. This alone might be beyond the capabilities of many lawyers. Even after the right analysis has been made and an alternative strategy and business model has been adopted, it still needs to be implemented. This might be beyond the capacity of many law firms, and as a consequence, they might face collapse. For those who make the transition, however, there is a bright future ahead.

ABOUT THE AUTHORS

Jaap Bosman is a leading strategy consultant and investor. He has over 15 years' experience in the legal sector and extensive international experience, including in China and Africa. In 2013, his international strategic achievements were recognized by the *Financial Times* with the first-ever Innovative Lawyers Award for International Strategy.

Jaap is a former member of the global Lex Mundi business development committee and the Lex Mundi marketing committee as well as a faculty member at the Cross Border Transactions Program of the Lex Mundi Institute in Monterey, California.

Jaap graduated with honors from Tilburg Law School. He also holds a degree as a qualified industrial designer. This unique combination of legal knowledge and applied creativity gives him the ability to devise truly innovative solutions. He was the first non-US person to receive the Thomson Reuters Hubbard One Excellence in Legal Marketing award.

Jaap is a cofounder and principal partner at TGO Consulting, a business strategy boutique for the legal sector. TGO Consulting operates from New York, The Hague, and Hong Kong and specializes in working with large and midsize business law firms (www.tgo-consulting.com).

Lisa Hakanson is a strategy consultant and business analyst. She has over a decade of experience in the legal sector and has worked internationally throughout her career. She was an in-house lawyer at one of the world's leading marine construction companies, with responsibility for high-value multiparty contracts for projects in the upstream oil and gas industry.

With strong research and analytical skills, Lisa has been working in the area of business development at the law firm side. She has been involved in strategic client development and market analysis and has conducted financial analysis.

Lisa graduated with honors in law from Stockholm University and holds an LL.M. cum laude in international business law.

Lisa is a cofounder and director at TGO Consulting, a business strategy boutique for the legal sector. TGO Consulting operates from New York, The Hague, and Hong Kong and specializes in working with large and midsize business law firms (www.tgo-consulting.com).

NOTES

Chapter 1

1. https://en.wikipedia.org/wiki/Brobeck,_Phleger_%26_Harrison.
2. Susan Beck, *Brobeck's Final Days*, THE AMERICAN LAWYER (2003, March 4).
3. Chambers & Partners, CHAMBERS GLOBAL: THE WORLD'S LEADING LAWYERS FOR BUSINESS (2009).
4. Peter Lattman, *Dewey & LeBoeuf Files for Bankruptcy*, NEW YORK TIMES (2012, May 28).
5. James B. Stewart, *The Collapse: How a Top Legal Firm Destroyed Itself*, THE NEW YORKER (2013, Oct. 14).
6. *Id.*
7. Although today we would find this description offensive, this is often the characteristic attributed to the original white-shoe firms. See for example http://wordnetweb.princeton.edu/perl/webwn?s=white-shoe and http://www.economist.com/blogs/johnson/2010/09/cliches.
8. *See* Elie Mystal, *Thelen Management Recommends Dissolution*, ABOVE THE LAW (2008, Oct. 28), http://legalpad.typepad.com/my_weblog/2008/10/thelen-launches-dissolution-vote.html.
9. Joshua Freedman, *Focus on SJ Berwin Merger Talks: Berwin in a China Shop*, THE LAWYER (2013, May 28).
10. Chris Johnson and Rose Walker, *King & Wood Mallesons: An Autopsy*, THE AMERICAN LAWYER (2016, December 12).

Chapter 2

1. Mergermarket, *Global and Regional M&A: Q1-Q4 2016* (2017, Jan. 4), http://www.mergermarket.com/pdf/MergermarketLegalLeagueTableReport.Q42016.pdf.
2. James Fontanella-Khan & Robin Wigglesworth, *US Dealmaking Hits $243bn Monthly Record*, FINANCIAL TIMES (June 1, 2015).

3. *The Global 100*, THE AMERICAN LAWYER (2016, Sept. 26), http://www.americanlawyer.com/id=1202767838452/The-Global-100.
4. See for example the report *Legal Services Global Market Analytics 2016*, THE BUSINESS RESEARCH COMPANY (November 2016) http://www.researchandmarkets.com/research/vhqjf8/legal_services.
5. TheCityUK, *UK Legal Services 2016: Legal Excellence, Internationally Renowned* (2016, July.), https://www.thecityuk.com/assets/2016/Reports-PDF/UK-Legal-services-2016.pdf.
6. Georgetown Law Center for the Study of the Legal Profession & Thomson Reuters Peer Monitor, *2016 Report on the State of the Legal Market* (2016), https://peermonitor.thomsonreuters.com/wp-content/uploads/2016/01/2016_PM_GT_Final-Report.pdf.
7. *See, e.g.*, Legal Executive Institute, *How Big Is the US Legal Services Market?* [Infographic], (2015), http://legalexecutiveinstitute.com/wp-content/uploads/2016/01/How-Big-is-the-US-Legal-Services-Market.pdf.
8. Pub. L. Order No. 43 (May 7, 2015) at 12, http://www.itcblog.com/images/order43in930.pdf.
9. TGO Consulting, *Mercenaries on the Move: An In-depth Analysis of Partner Mobility in the German Legal Market* (2016).
10. *The Lateral Report: Moves Hit a Post-Recession High*, THE AMERICAN LAWYER (2016, Feb. 1).
11. Motive Legal Consulting, *Lateral Partner Moves in London, Year IV, Annual Survey 2006–2013* (2014, March), http://www.motivelegal.com/wp-content/uploads/downloads/Motive_LateralResearch_March2014.pdf.
12. *Attack of the bean-counters*, THE ECONOMIST (2015, March 19) http://www.economist.com/news/business/21646741-lawyers-beware-accountants-are-coming-after-your-business-attack-bean-counters.
13. Judy Triedman, *Deloitte, Other Accounting Giants, See Legal Services Growth*, LAW.COM (2016, Sept. 9), http://www.law.com/sites/almstaff/2016/09/09/deloitte-other-accounting-giants-see-legal-services-growth/?slreturn=20170110091242.
14. Legal Executive Institute, *supra* note 7.
15. Carl Benedikt Frey & Michael A. Osborne, *The Future of Employment: How Susceptible Are Jobs to Computerisation?*, Oxford Martin Programme on the Impacts of Future Technology (2013), http://www.oxfordmartin.ox.ac.uk/downloads/academic/The_Future_of_Employment.pdf.
16. *Id.* at 40.
17. Shelly Tan, *Job Terminator: Can Robots Learn Your Skills?*, WASHINGTON POST (2015, June 27), https://www.washingtonpost.com/graphics/health/watson-jobs.

Chapter 3

1. *The Global 100*, THE AMERICAN LAWYER (2016, Sept. 26), http://www.americanlawyer.com/id=1202767838452/The-Global-100.
2. Joanne Harris, The art of survival, The Lawyer European 100 - 2013, THE LAWYER (2013).
3. Legal Executive Institute, *How Big Is the US Legal Services Market?* [Infographic], (2015), http://legalexecutiveinstitute.com/wp-content/uploads/2016/01/How-Big-is-the-US-Legal-Services-Market.pdf.
4. *Supra* note 1.
5. Global Legal Post and TerraLex, *The General Counsel Excellence Report 2015: US Edition*, http://www.globallegalpost.com/publications/9a77a2aed4ae52d363f713c02ea42742.
6. CCP Research Foundation, *Conduct Costs Project Report 2015* (2016, July). http://conductcosts.ccpresearchfoundation.com/conduct-costs-results
7. TheCityUK, *UK Legal Services 2016: Legal Excellence, Internationally Renowned* (2016, July), https://www.thecityuk.com/assets/2016/Reports-PDF/UK-Legal-services-2016.pdf.
8. Joanne Harris, *Germany – Crossing borders*, THE LAWYER (2014, July 28)
9. Rachel E. Stern & Su Li, *The Outpost Office: How International Law Firms Approach the China Market*, 41 LAW & SOCIAL INQUIRY 184–211 (2016).
10. *China Elite 2015 report*, THE LAWYER (2015).
11. Official list of foreign law firms in China 2014: P.R.C. Ministry of Justice Bulletin No. 156, http://www.moj.gov.cn/lsgzgzzds/content/2015-08/14/content_6221286_4.htm. Official list of foreign law firms in China 2013: P.R.C. Ministry of Justice Bulletin No. 147, http://www.moj.gov.cn/index/content/2014-08/13/content_5718054.htm?node=7346.SeealsoYunKriegler, *Chinese market sees drop in international firms for first time ever*, THE LAWYER (2015, October 6) https://www.thelawyer.com/issues/online-october-2015/chinese-market-sees-drop-in-international-firms-for-first-time-ever.

Chapter 4

1. Tabby Kinder, *Exclusive: Exclusive: Shell Hires Pricing Analyst to Manage Fees ahead of Panel Review*, THE LAWYER (2015, May 22), https://www.thelawyer.com/issues/online-may-2015/exclusive-shell-hires-pricing-analyst-to-manage-fees-ahead-of-panel-review.

Chapter 6

1. Peter Lattman, *Culture Keeps Firms Together in Trying Times*, NEW YORK TIMES (2012, May 25).

2. Simon Kuper, *Something in the way she speaks*, THE FINANCIAL TIMES (2011, June 24).
3. https://www.cravath.com/cravathsystem.
4. *Informal Innovation: Entrepreneurship and Informal Communities*, The Economist Intelligence Unit (2016, November) http://informalinnovation.economist.com/?utm_source=PR&utm_medium=email&utm_content=IMDA.
5. Pui-Guan Man, *Slaughters moves to merit-based pay to reward exceptional associates*, LEGAL WEEK (2013, January 17).
6. Rob Asghar, *What Millennials Want In The Workplace (And Why You Should Start Giving It To Them)*, FORBES (2014, January 13). For the Cassandra Report see https://cassandra.co.
7. *Id.*

Chapter 7

1. Lindsay Fortado, *British Firms Borrow Record Sums to Expand*, FINANCIAL TIMES (2015, Aug. 16), https://www.ft.com/content/234dd5f2-440f-11e5-b3b2-1672f710807b.
2. Jacqueline Palank, *Howrey Partners Are Assailed on the Law Firm's Demise*, WALL STREET JOURNAL (2013, March 25).

Chapter 8

1. http://www.margaretthatcher.org/archive/1984cac1.asp.
2. United States, Training Within Industry Service. Training Within Industry Materials: Bulletins Issued by Training Within Industry and Outlines of the Training Within Industry Programs for War Plants and Essential Services (1945).
3. Jim Huntzinger, *The Roots of Lean—Training Within Industry: The Origin of Japanese Management and Kaizen* (no date), http://www.lean.org/Search/Documents/105.pdf.

Chapter 9

1. A. H. Maslow, *A Theory of Human Motivation*, 50 PSYCHOLOGICAL REVIEW 370-96 (1943), at 383.
2. http://www.myersbriggs.org/my-mbti-personality-type/mbti-basics.
3. Lucy Kellaway, *It's Time to Sack Job Appraisals*, FINANCIAL TIMES (2010, July 11), https://www.ft.com/content/a72a8ca6-8b8e-11df-ab4d-00144feab49a.
4. *Id.*

5. Lillian Cunningham, *In Big Move, Accenture Will Get Rid of Annual Performance Reviews and Rankings*, Washington Post (2015, July 21).
6. Lillian Cunningham, *Accenture's CEO Explains Why He's Overhauling Performance Reviews*, Washington Post (2015, July 23).

Chapter 10

1. John Hagel, John Seely Brown, Tamara Samoylova, & Matt Frost, *The Burdens of the Past: Report 4 of the 2013 Shift Index Series* (2013, Nov. 11), https://dupress.deloitte.com/dup-us-en/topics/emerging-technologies/the-burdens-of-the-past.html.
2. William D. Henderson, Three Generations of U.S. Lawyers: Generalists, Specialists, Project Managers, p. 378, Maurer School of Law: Indiana University (2011) https://pdfs.semanticscholar.org/06c5/6e86dcb891c6545ca440fac6ab6a12a10acf.pdf.
3. Georgetown Law Center for the Study of the Legal Profession & Thomson Reuters Peer Monitor, *2016 Report on the State of the Legal Market* (2016), https://peermonitor.thomsonreuters.com/wp-content/uploads/2016/01/2016_PM_GT_Final-Report.pdf.
4. *See, e.g.*, Rene Reich-Graefe, *Keep Calm and Carry On*, 27 Geo. J. Legal Ethics (2014), https://papers.ssrn.com/sol3/papers.cfm?abstract_id=2404603.
5. Georgetown Law Center for the Study of the Legal Profession & Thomson Reuters Peer Monitor, *2014 Report on the State of the Legal Market* (2014), at 13, https://peermonitor.thomsonreuters.com/wp-content/uploads/2014/01/2014_PM_GT_Report5.pdf.
6. Clay Christensen, Dina Wang, & Derek C. M. van Bever, *Consulting on the Cusp of Disruption*, 91 Harv. Bus. Rev. 10 (2013).
7. Georgetown Law Center for the Study of the Legal Profession & Thomson Reuters Peer Monitor, *2015 Report on the State of the Legal Market* (2015), http://www.law.georgetown.edu/academics/centers-institutes/legal-profession/upload/FINAL-Report-1-7-15.pdf.

INDEX